Motivating Professors to Teach Effectively

Norwich

James L. Bess, *Editor*

NEW DIRECTIONS FOR TEACHING AND LEARNING

KENNETH E. EBLE and JOHN F. NOONAN, *Editors-in-Chief*

Number 10, June 1982

Paperback sourcebooks in
The Jossey-Bass Higher Education Series

Jossey-Bass Inc., Publishers
San Francisco • Washington • London

Motivating Professors to Teach Effectively
Number 10, June 1982
    James L. Bess, *Editor*

New Directions for Teaching and Learning Series
Kenneth E. Eble and John F. Noonan, *Editors-in-Chief*

New Directions for Teaching and Learning is published quarterly
by Jossey-Bass Inc., Publishers. Subscriptions, single-issue
orders, change of address notices, undelivered copies, and other
correspondence should be sent to *New Directions* Subscriptions,
Jossey-Bass Inc., Publishers, 433 California Street, San Francisco,
California 94104.

Editorial correspondence should be sent to the Editors-in-Chief,
Kenneth E. Eble or John F. Noonan, Center for Improving
Teaching Effectiveness, Virginia Commonwealth University,
Richmond, Virginia 23284.

Library of Congress Catalogue Card Number LC 81-48583
International Standard Serial Number ISSN 0271-0633
International Standard Book Number ISBN 87589-924-2

Cover art by Willi Baum
Manufactured in the United States of America

Ordering Information

The paperback sourcebooks listed below are published quarterly and can be ordered either by subscription or as single copies.

Subscriptions cost $35.00 per year for institutions, agencies, and libraries. Individuals can subscribe at the special rate of $21.00 per year *if payment is by personal check.* (Note that the full rate of $35.00 applies if payment is by institutional check, even if the subscription is designated for an individual.) Standing orders are accepted.

Single copies are available at $7.95 when payment accompanies order, and *all single-copy orders under $25.00 must include payment.* (California, Washington, D.C., New Jersey, and New York residents please include appropriate sales tax.) For billed orders, cost per copy is $7.95 plus postage and handling. (Prices subject to change without notice.)

To ensure correct and prompt delivery, all orders must give either the *name of an individual* or an *official purchase order number.* Please submit your order as follows:

Subscriptions: specify series and subscription year.
Single Copies: specify sourcebook code and issue number (such as, TL8).

Mail orders for United States and Possessions, Latin America, Canada, Japan, Australia, and New Zealand to:
Jossey-Bass Inc., Publishers
433 California Street
San Francisco, California 94104

Mail orders for all other parts of the world to:
Jossey-Bass Limited
28 Banner Street
London EC1Y 8QE

New Directions for Teaching and Learning Series
Kenneth E. Eble and John F. Noonan, *Editors-in-Chief*

Contents

Expectancy theory, an approach to motivation that has been extensively applied to industrial situations, can be used in the college or university setting. It predicts that faculty members will be motivated to teach when they believe that effort devoted to teaching will lead to effective classroom performance and that performance will lead to the attainment of valued outcomes. Implications are discussed with respect to how institutions of higher education can increase faculty motivation to teach.

Organizational Structure

Grouping teaching tasks into self-contained roles and developing richer lateral relations, better information systems, and clearer teaching goals may better match faculty needs for autonomy and improve their motivation to teach.

Over the past ten years, researchers have made considerable progress in discovering how to design feedback systems that can help improve university teaching. This chapter suggests that the congruence of the design and the organizational context has an important effect on the effectiveness of a feedback system.

Research Note and Summary

The research literature and theory are examined for evidence to support a contention that faculty have distinct career phases for any of their traditional roles. Whether or not faculty pass through extended phases in their motivation to teach remains an open question.

Improving motivation to teach depends on the identification of rewards which are significant and meaningful to faculty and on an intelligent system for making those rewards available.

Editor's Notes

In common sense terms, most of us place a strong positive value on having people "motivated." We assume that a motivated person is in some sense more psychologically healthy and that organizations comprised of motivated persons are in some ways better off. We also make a connection between motivation and effort. That is, we say that when a person is motivated, he or she is likely to engage in some activity. Frequently, we assume that the activity has positive consequences for both individual and organization. As energy is expended, work gets done, in turn causing a reciprocal return of energy to the actor. Thus, when a faculty member teaches, we assume that, although there has been some dissipation of energy—transmission of heat, light, and information—there is an ultimate return of energy, in different form, to both individual and organization. The energy returns in tangible and intangible forms, and in immediate and instrumental ways.

A faculty member may be rejuvenated by the proximate situation in which the energy is returned almost at once by his or her students. Metaphorically, the faculty member's energy is "reflected" back from the student; more philosophically, faculty and student energies are conjoined, in shared knowledge, ways of thinking, attitudes, and values. Alternatively, the faculty member may find the energy exchange balanced in an almost solipsistic way—the physical energy going out releases simultaneously the kinetic energy stored within. The process of engaging in the activity itself creates a feedback loop which is only partially dependent on outside conditions. Still another form is the energy returned to the faculty member *after* the teaching act—in the form of "chits" which the faculty member can cash in later. Salary checks, for example, may be used to buy other pleasures, faculty status may earn respect, and knowledge gained can be banked for later use.

Energy is also a useful concept in understanding an apparent lack of motivation. To characterize a person as "unmotivated" is often to stigmatize a situation which needs to be understood in more neutral terms. When we say a person is unmotivated to perform a task, we imply an unwillingness or inability to perceive opportunities for equivalent energy exchange. The person perceives the task performance as requiring more effort than it will return in psychic or instrumental energy units. The unmotivated person, then, is simply one for whom this particular situation is not an opportunity. Some argue that for many people, past experience has taught them that no organizational situations can or do provide adequate opportunities. Hence, the expenditure of minimally acceptable energy is seen as not worthwhile under virtually any conditions.

.

1

Both people and organizations have a number of ways of dealing with organizational settings. The most common is for organizations to recruit and hire people who are likely to find the field in general, and the organization in particular, as having sufficient and sustained opportunities for expending energy with an expectation of return. Enlightened organizations continually work at structuring those opportunities and at infusing them with value, as Selznick (1957) notes. Other organizations assume, in varying degrees, either that individuals are intransigently incapable of perceiving opportunities or that the work to be done is inherently distasteful. Under these assumptions (that is, when the psychic returns from the work itself are not forthcoming — or allegedly not forthcoming), organizations must import extra energy from outside to increase the worker's perceived balance of input to output. They must either pay more in instrumental energy units, or they must exert more energy in control and supervision. Unmotivated workers are thus seen as deleterious to the efficiency and effectiveness of the system.

In these externally constrained settings, the unmotivated person who wishes to remain in the system must make accommodations to it. The person must either conform to the demands of the situation or exert physical and psychic energy in avoiding conformity. Both choices require the output of energy in excess of the expected return, but most people have defense mechanisms which prevent their seeing how "expensive," in psychic energy terms, both conformity to minimal standards and avoidance of work are. Moreover, where organizational leverage on behavior is low (as in loosely coupled academic systems), persons can both not conform and not expend much effort in fending off demands for performance.

The main concern of this volume is the extent to which institutions of higher education represent viable opportunities for academic workers. The degree that faculty can be expected to perceive continuing opportunities for receiving "just" returns in exchange for their work is considered. It is evident that there are small numbers of faculty who are dispositionally insouciant or who have been able to strike a balance between energy expended and energy returned. These productive scholars and teachers continue to be willing to devote time and energy which is beneficial to their institution's clients as well as to themselves. This admirable synergy may not, however, apply to most faculty, and it certainly varies among all faculty as age and career stages unfold, as the perception of opportunities waxes and wanes over the life cycle.

There is an increasing proportion of faculty who are constrained to remain at their institutions instead of, as in former times, seeking what seem to be greener pastures. Many of the following chapters address this phenomenon of economic or organizational incarceration. If we are to believe Walton (1980), we may expect to see increasing numbers of faculty shifting from positive moral and spontaneous expressive involvement to calculative and alienative involvement. In place of positive affect and enjoyment, we will see neutrality or low — if not negative — affect, as many faculty turn away from or against their institutions. Strong faculty needs for autonomy are pressed when there are constraints on the right to choose environments conducive to perceived changing needs and competences.

The sense of constraint on one's life, to which faculty are largely unaccustomed, has a chilling effect on the perception of opportunities in the environment. Faculty tend to associate the vicissitudes of their life-stage changes with the institution. Instead of recognizing the changes within themselves, they tend to shift the locus of causality to their environments. As Deci and Ryan point out in their chapter, such an external attribution is reinforced by the decline in slack resources in most institutions. Thus, while the opportunities for energy returns from teaching have probably not declined at all, many faculty will increasingly see themselves enervated by the teaching environment. They will allege it has become both more routine and less under their control. The work of teaching may and should involve some risking of energy capital against a hoped-for but not always forthcoming return.

There are many "conditions of teaching" (Bess, 1977), however, which interrupt the communications and energy exchanges necessary for sustained faculty motivation and risk taking. Among these are the difficulties associated with the various tasks of teaching. The translation of raw knowledge into an instructional activity by a faculty member requires insight into the meaning of a liberal education, the dynamics of lecturing or leading discussions, and the psychology of learning. Any conscientious faculty member must struggle against the tendency to view course and class objectives as merely the achievement by most students of a passing grade on a final examination or paper. It is little wonder that the typical faculty member finds it necessary to make oversimplified assumptions about what the teaching task ought to be. As a consequence, the richness and variety of satisfying opportunities from the teaching effort are not generally perceived. Energy is expended on the safe and the known.

Not only is the technology of the teaching task complex (Perrow, 1970), but the teaching role is often ambiguous and conflictive. Mixed messages from both formal and informal sources communicate inadequately what is expected from faculty, and what effort is expected to be devoted to the activity. Demands in wide variety and strength are made on faculty time, and even within the teaching sub-role, the input-output energy exchanges are uncertain. When no one knows what good education is, when no one knows what good teaching is, when no one knows how to tell when good teaching has taken place, and when no one knows how one is supposed to feel as a successful teacher, the interpretation of the role is left almost entirely to the individual faculty member. Given the rather strong proscriptions against sharing either success or failure at teaching, it is little wonder that the faculty member loses faith in the classroom as an opportunity for reward and satisfaction.

What we commonly find in academia, then, is a not unexpected increase in protective and defensive behavior among most faculty. Originally, at least, faculty are enthusiastic about the prospects of transmitting their excitement about their recently acquired knowledge as graduate students. They soon discover, for the reasons noted previously, that teaching is confusing, and, subsequently, that due to its confusion, teaching is insufficiently rewarding, anxiety producing, and tiring. A typical reaction is to circumscribe their goals and expectations. Faculty learn to expect less from the teaching activity and to put less effort into it. This reaction is condoned by peers who have gone through similar withdrawal transitions. As time goes on, faculty develop habits of not seeing teaching as an opportunity and of therefore not seeking to capitalize on that opportunity.

These habits are not countered by inherent dispositions which might be expected to be present in persons attracted to working in colleges and universities. Academics typically are not predisposed to seek and find satisfactions in teaching. Many have drifted into the profession out of love for research and knowledge acquisition — a task which requires that they put up with long periods of isolated behavior, at least, and that they enjoy it, at best. Thus, academicians are generally not predisposed to enjoy the social interaction which is central to teaching and learning. Once committed to the profession, they encounter teaching tasks about which they know little or nothing and which they find difficult and frustrating to perform. Faculty get little peer support, either in a practical or an emotional sense. Few significant others help them learn to teach or overcome their anxieties and frustrations, as still fewer demonstrate as role models the joys of teaching. Along with mass higher education have come new kinds of students whose skills and intellectual orientations are so different from those of faculty that a distance, if not antipathy, is likely to develop. Finally, along with reduced budgets come administrators whose positions as former faculty members have not afforded them much insight into the energy input-output balance — save as fellow sufferers. Now, forced to reallocate resources in response to pressures from many external sources and faced with a heavily tenured faculty, these administrators look to the development of incentives to induce faculty to perform tasks seen as burdensome, not fulfilling.

The authors of the following chapters clearly have recognized these dilemmas. Their concern is with the development of conceptual frameworks which will help faculty and administrators to understand the causes of these dilemmas and to develop enlightened policies to improve teaching. To attempt to synthesize their perspectives is difficult; some are in obvious conflict. To a degree, that is inevitable, considering the surprisingly sparse amount of empirical research extant on faculty motivation. It is hoped, however, that these disparate approaches will provide useful insights.

The structure of the chapter offerings is fairly straightforward and is conveyed well by the chapter headings. McKeachie's chapter sets out the central problems of academic life today and poses the controversy over the utility of intrinsic versus extrinsic rewards. Csikszentmihalyi explores the inner life of a rewarded and motivated person, while Deci and Ryan consider the interactive effects of intrinsic and extrinsic rewards. With a focus on the internal — or intrinsic — sources of motivation, Schneider and Zalesny examine the need structure of the typical academic. The force of cognitively recognized rewards and the probabilities of achieving them form the core of Mowday's chapter, while Nord presents the case for the use of behavior modification techniques for the improvement of teaching. The last three chapters examine not individuals but environmental conditions which might affect the motivation to teach — Blackburn on the academic career, Hall and Bazerman on organizational design, and Cammann on feedback systems.

James L. Bess
Editor

References

Bess, J. L. "The Motivation to Teach." *Journal of Higher Education,* 1977, *48* (1), 243–258.
Perrow, C. *Organizational Analysis: A Sociological View.* Belmont, Calif.: Wadsworth Publishing Company, 1970.
Selznick, P. *Leadership in Administration.* New York: Harper & Row, 1957.
Walton, R. E. "Establishing and Maintaining High Commitment Work Systems." In J. R. Kimberly, R. H. Miles, and Associates (Eds.), *The Organizational Life Cycle.* San Francisco: Jossey-Bass, 1980.

James L. Bess is professor of higher education, New York University. His recently published book, University Organization, *deals with the accommodation of faculty and institutional interests.*

Increased emphasis upon competition, tightened administrative controls, and evaluation reduce efficiency rather than improve it.

The Rewards of Teaching

W. J. McKeachie

Two years ago I wrote a chapter on academic motivation entitled "Financial Incentives Are Ineffective for Faculty" (Lewis and Becker, 1979). While that title was something of an overstatement, it does indicate a direction that the present chapter will take, since what I propose to do is to add some afterthoughts with respect to faculty motivation for teaching. Before doing so, I shall review the arguments presented in the earlier chapter for the benefit of those who missed them, or have by now forgotten them.

In my earlier work, I pointed out that there is a good deal of evidence that extrinsic incentives such as money are likely to have undesirable long-term effects on motivation, since one must increasingly raise the ante if one is to maintain motivation. Research indicates that when one suffers an extrinsic incentive for something that otherwise is enjoyable for its own sake, one's motivation to continue that activity drops. I argued that most individuals entering college and university teaching have not done so in order to attain high salaries or other extrinsic rewards, but primarily because of the enjoyment they receive from scholarly pursuits, stimulation from colleagues and students, and the satisfactions of being appreciated and respected by others. I reviewed a number of studies of faculty motivation suggesting that faculty members find their positions intrinsically satisfying in terms of complexity,

The author gratefully acknowledges the help of conversations with Professor Donald Brown and other colleagues at the Center for Research on Learning and Teaching.

J. Bess (Ed.). *New Directions for Teaching and Learning: Motivating Professors to Teach Effectively*, no. 10. San Francisco: Jossey-Bass, June 1982.

responsibility for other persons, autonomy, and interpersonal relationships. One evidence of the general importance of these intrinsic satisfactions is the freedom of academicians from cardiovascular diseases associated with high levels of stress. Placing heavy emphasis upon salary increases, making promotions to tenure more difficult and competitive, and putting a strong emphasis on external evaluation for rewards and punishments are all likely to decrease the effectiveness of teaching by faculty members over their lifetime. If we wish to increase effectiveness we need to consider ways of increasing the intrinsic satisfactions found in teaching.

Changes Threatening Motivation for Teaching

Since I wrote the chapter for the Lewis and Becker book, a number of changes have occurred in the state of American higher education which seem to me ominous for teaching effectiveness.

First is the decline of professors' salaries in relationship to those of other professions. Second is the change in the academic marketplace, with greater emphasis on research and scholarly productivity as a criterion for promotion and much greater competitiveness among young people striving to achieve tenure. Third is the increased tendency, as budgets tighten, to centralize more and more decisions in higher-level administration and to place increasing restrictions upon the autonomy of individual faculty members. Fourth is increased emphasis upon evaluation. Each of these conditions seems to me likely to be an important source of loss of intrinsic satisfaction. Together they are likely to result in a loss of quality of education over time. Let us examine each in turn.

Salaries Are Not Important, But Low Salaries Are Bad. My emphasis upon intrinsic motivation does not mean that salaries and promotions are not important. I argued in the Lewis and Becker volume, as I still do, that when salaries fall significantly below one's expectations (particularly if one's salary lags behind salaries of colleagues whom one perceives to be peers), dissatisfaction and a corrosion of one's enthusiasm and commitment can result. Effective teachers often feel that they are falling behind individuals contributing only through research or other activities that are less significant than teaching. The result may be resentment and bitterness which eventually interfere with effective teaching.

Salary increases and promotions are part of a social system. In this system, salaries are not so much important in their own right or in terms of what they will buy but rather for what they symbolize in terms of one's status and prestige among colleagues. Similarly, being promoted indicates the achievement of competence in the eyes of respected peers. This is no small part of the sense of satisfaction in one's work.

However, heavy emphasis upon salaries and promotions as incentives may paradoxically result in poorer, rather than better, university teaching. If individuals publish research papers and spend time on teaching largely because they see this as important to promotion, what happens once the promotion has been achieved? Presumably, college or university administrators must provide an unending series of promotions and pay increases if productivity is to be maintained. Otherwise, the individual will look for other activities that are similarly rewarding. We see evidence of this sort of motivation in the tendency to devise super-ranks, named chairs, or other devices providing additional marks of distinction beyond the usual academic ranks of assistant professor, associate professor, and professor. Without such rewards and with little intrinsic motivation, effectiveness drops.

Competition Leads Not to Survival, But to Extinction of Motivation. There is no inherent conflict between research and teaching in the teaching profession. To be good teachers, we must be learners ourselves, modeling for students the intellectual curiosity and disciplined inquiry we hope to teach. Published research may provide evidence of the quality of mind and spirit we desire, but it is only one sort of evidence. The lack or existence of published research does not prove the lack or existence of these desired qualities. In making decisions about awarding tenure, one looks for predictors about the contribution of individuals throughout their careers. One wants to promote people who are enthralled by their research, who enjoy teaching, who have such enthusiasm for their work that the external rewards are simply incidental indicators of recognition rather than goals in themselves.

A heavy emphasis upon competing with one's peers to achieve higher student ratings or a longer list of publications risks the promotion of individuals who are not strongly motivated for teaching or research for its own sake but who, instead, teach effectively or publish prodigiously primarily in order to achieve promotion. The habits of competition—of guarding ideas from peers, of downgrading colleagues' teaching or research in order to exalt one's own—may persist and destroy the collegiality and sense of peer support which have been found by Caplan and others (1975) to be an important source of faculty satisfaction. Increased concern about promotion to tenure by young faculty members may result in a productivity drop following promotion to tenure, rather than a freeing of energy and a relief from tension. Working primarily to achieve intrinsic rewards—competing against one's peers—may not be effective when career development depends upon cooperative collegial relations based on mutual commitment to one's college and discipline. Increased competition for tenure may result in a less productive, rather than more productive, tenured faculty.

Tightening Administrative Controls Reduces Efficiency. As I indicated earlier, studies of faculty motivation indicate that one of the major sources of faculty satisfaction is a feeling of autonomy—a sense of being able to exert a good deal of personal control over one's time and energy. Because of a sense of personal control, faculty members typically spend much more than forty hours a week in planning and preparing classes, counseling students, and pursuing their scholarly endeavors. The work is fun because it is chosen; the same work carried out in response to orders from others becomes burdensome and unpleasant.

As budgets tighten, the natural administrative reaction is to tighten up on the looseness in academic life. Courses offered because of faculty interests are eliminated, variations in teaching load are reduced, and irregular hours of work are frowned upon. In order to achieve the ends of education more efficiently, the means become more and more prescribed and the result is a loss, rather than increase, of efficiency because faculty members no longer go beyond the formal requirements (see Deci and Ryan's chapter, this volume).

Research on achievement motivation indicates that independence is one characteristic of individuals high in the need for Achievement. Such individuals seek and are most highly motivated in situations permitting independent effort. As Schneider and Zalesny suggest in their chapter in this volume, college professors have typically been selected because of previous success in achievement, and we would thus expect them to teach best when the situation gives them opportunities to develop methods which create a sense of achieving high standards by their own problem solving and creativity.

Negative Rather Than Positive Effects of Increased Emphasis on Evaluation. As budgets tighten and colleges and universities come under increased public scrutiny, the tendency is to put greater emphasis on "accountability." Colleges and universities develop more formal and systematic systems of evaluation; annual reviews are made of each individual's progress; productivity is evaluated each year. Such stress on evaluation is a natural consequence of the current pressures. Evaluation is undertaken with the expectation that establishing clear mechanisms for administering salary increases, promotions, and other rewards or punishments will result in improved effectiveness. Stating that there should be clear standards for evaluation seems almost as noncontroversial as motherhood and apple pie, yet as I have indicated earlier (McKeachie, 1975), and as March (1980) has suggested more cogently, there is a big difference between maximum clarity and optimal clarity of standards. While there are, no doubt, some positive outcomes from emphasizing evaluation, there may also be unintended negative consequences. One of the effects of evaluation is to arouse anxiety. While we have few, if any, studies of faculty anxieties, we have a great many studies of anxiety about achievement among children and college students. We know that anxiety is likely to have a damaging effect upon performance. Individuals who become anxious under the threat of evaluation are likely to be less creative, more rigid, less effective in solving problems, and to display more superficial, less effective methods of learning and processing information.

Assuming that these results also apply to faculty members, we might expect that heavy emphasis on evaluation would result in performance designed to meet external standards. Articles will be published on conventional topics that can be addressed quickly to achieve frequent publications. Teaching is likely to be characterized by strong organization and methods that meet conventional standards. Heavy emphasis on evaluation may serve to reduce poor teaching resulting from inadequate preparation and inattention to the responsibilities of teaching. However, it is also likely to result in less innovation, less emphasis on long-term outcomes of education, and, most important, less enthusiasm and commitment of the kind of extraordinary time and effort characterizing individuals who enjoy teaching and who are wrapped up in the enjoyable complexities of determining the best methods for teaching a particular subject matter to a particular group of students.

Motivation and Teaching Improvement

Current theories of development of the self suggest that one of the most important aspects of personality for most individuals is a sense of self-competence and self-efficacy. One of the reasons that faculty development programs are particularly important in these critical times for higher education is that if we are to nurture intrinsic satisfactions in teaching, we need to help both young and old teachers develop a greater sense of self-competency and self-efficacy; that is, we need to help them carry out their course planning and carry on their classroom activities with a sense that they are doing them well. We need also to help faculty be sensitive to cues that give them a sense that students are learning and are interested. Thus, to the degree that we can help faculty members develop additional skills in teaching so that they have a repertoire of techniques and methods to draw upon, we are likely to increase the faculty members' satisfaction in teaching.

Similarly, to the degree that we can help faculty members become more aware of student reactions and provide mechanisms such as student ratings to give faculty members a sense of student opinions which are useful for course improvement and for judging students' interest and motivation, we can contribute to a faculty member's increased sense that specific teaching efforts are paying off.

Research evidence indicates that when one encounters a discrepancy between one's self-theory and other evidence, there is motivation to do something. When one receives poor student ratings, the threat to self may be so great that one tries to avoid teaching or to defend against the threat by denying the validity of the student judgments, or by retreating to the most conventional and minimally involving kinds of teaching. However, when moderate discrepancies exist and one's sense of self-competence includes the hope of improvement, motivation to change may result in greater effectiveness. (For evidence, see Centra, 1973.)

In short, intrinsic satisfactions are not necessarily ones that come automatically or come easily. In fact, it may well be that one of the reasons that teachers continue to be fascinated by teaching is that the rewards are never certain and that the task of teaching continues to reveal unsolved problems.

12

How Can One Enhance Intrinsic Satisfactions for Teaching?

We have suggested that intrinsic satisfactions are derived from such things as satisfying relationships with students and colleagues, from intellectual stimulation, and from a sense of freedom and autonomy in carrying out one's job with a sense of personal control and efficacy. The measures needed for enhancing motivation are therefore almost self-evident. For example, to increase satisfactions from observing student growth and development and establishing personal relationships with students, it is clear that small classes, in which there are many opportunities to get to know students, are important. If one is to observe growth in students and have the satisfaction of attributing some of that growth to one's own teaching, opportunities for working with students over long periods of time—longer than a typical one-term course—are likely to be important.

Talking with colleagues about teaching is a simple thing, but relatively rare on most college campuses. Our own Center for Research on Learning and Teaching sponsors a weekly brown-bag luncheon of faculty members who enjoy discussing their teaching. Conducting many such informal meetings could be a powerful force for increasing the satisfaction of teaching.

Providing choices in terms of courses to be taught, organization of course materials, and distribution of work load throughout the year are techniques of enhancing one's sense of personal control and can be implemented without loss of departmental efficiency. The psychology department at the University of Michigan for many years has asked each faculty member some months in advance to indicate the teaching and other assignments he or she would prefer for the coming term. Such preferences can be honored in over 90 percent of the cases, since most faculty members are relatively well informed about the needs of the department and are able to meet those needs doing things that they enjoy, or at least do not resent. Such a system contrasts with one in which the activities of faculty members are strongly constrained by decisions made by department chairpersons or other administrators as to standard work loads, standard course syllabi, and so on.

Finally, as Mowday (in this volume) suggests, opportunities for faculty members to increase their sense of competence and of growing effectiveness can be provided through workshops, microteaching, and opportunities to consult with supportive and nonevaluative colleagues who are willing to provide suggestions about methods of teaching, handling difficult students, and other problems as they arise. If the department is so large that department members do not easily find a colleague to provide such consultation, the department might arrange for one or more consultants to be officially designated as available for advice and counsel on the problems of teaching.

The teaching profession is more than a science, more than an art, more than a craft. It involves all of these together with commitment—commitment to one's students, one's discipline, and to the ever challenging task of getting ideas and motives out of the mind of the teacher and course materials into the mind and spirit of the student.

References

Caplan, R. D., Cobb, S., French, J. R. P., Harrison, R. V., and Pinneau, S. R., Jr. *Job Demands and Worker Health.* Washington, D.C.: U.S. Government Printing Office, 1975.

Centra, J. A. "Effectiveness of Student Feedback in Modifying College Instruction." *Journal of Educational Psychology,* 1973, *65,* 395–401.

Lewis, D. R., and Becker, W. E., Jr. (Eds.). *Academic Rewards in Higher Education.* Cambridge, Mass.: Ballinger, 1979.

McKeachie, W. J. "The Decline and Fall of the Laws of Learning." *Educational Researcher,* 1975, *3* (3), 7–11.

McKeachie, W. J. "Financial Incentives Are Ineffective for Faculty." In Lewis, D. R., and Becker, W. E., Jr. (Eds.), *Academic Rewards in Higher Education.* Cambridge: Ballinger, 1979.

March, J. G. *How We Talk and How We Act: Administrative Theory and Administrative Life.* Urbana: University of Illinois, 1980.

Wilbert J. McKeachie is professor of psychology and director of the Center for Research on Learning and Teaching at the University of Michigan. A past president of the American Psychological Association, he has devoted his research and teaching career to problems of university teaching.

The products of teaching are students who enjoy learning;
the means for accomplishing this goal are teachers who are
intrinsically motivated to learn.

Intrinsic Motivation and Effective Teaching: A Flow Analysis

Mihaly Czikszentmihalyi

There is a great deal of confusion concerning teaching at the university level. Labeling it "teaching" and those who do it "teachers" does not help either. To teach implies a transfer of information, and that is not the main purpose of higher education. In fact, those who teach in universities are called "professors," because their primary function is to profess an intellectual discipline. The most relevant meaning of the act of professing is the Middle English connotation of being bound by a vow or, the even older Latin one that refers to confessing one's faith in, or expressing allegiance to, some idea or goal.

Thus, at least originally and ideally, an effective university teacher is one who believes in what he or she does to the point of identifying with it. In my opinion this view does not simply reflect a quaint historical or etymological curiosity. It continues to represent the most important contribution that teachers at a university can make to the education of their students. Higher education succeeds or fails in terms of motivation, not cognitive transfer of information. It succeeds if it instills in students a willingness to pursue knowledge for its own sake; it fails if students learn simply in order to get a degree. The best way to get students to believe that it makes sense to pursue knowledge is to believe in it oneself. Thus, an effective professor is one who is intrinsically

J. Bess (Ed.). *New Directions for Teaching and Learning: Motivating Professors to Teach Effectively*, no. 10. San Francisco: Jossey-Bass, June 1982.

motivated to learn, because it is he or she who will have the best chance to educate others.

When we try to improve the organizational design of schools, change its reward contingencies and feedback systems (see chapters by Cammann; Hall and Bazerman; and by Nord, this volume) we are essentially trying to bring the behavior of teachers in line with some a priori criterion of effectiveness. These attempts are useful for improving the teaching component of a professor's job, but they tend to leave the more essential professing component unaffected. In fact, such attempts might make an allegiance to knowledge for its own sake more unlikely. It may be difficult for an intelligent human being to identify with an institution run by administrators whose main question is: "How can environmental conditions be developed so as to increase the frequency and intensity of 'good' teaching?" (as Nord suggests in his chapter that they should be). From what we know, it is clear that external control and manipulation of this sort will destroy intrinsic motivation (see chapters by Deci and Ryan; and by McKeachie, this volume). Thus, we might safely conclude that efforts to improve teaching which result in a professor's attributing to an outside agency control over his or her action will lead to the exact opposite outcome from the one intended (that is, to inefficient education due to a loss of a professor's intrinsic motivation).

The Loss of Intrinsic Motivation

Before developing this argument further, it might be worthwhile to clarify a few points concerning intrinsic motivation. The importance of this concept is not so much that motivation is an efficient means toward some outside goal — such as good teaching, learning, or making more money — but that such motivation reflects an experience that is an end in itself — a dynamic psychological state that is valued for its immediate rewarding qualities.

In most cultures, and especially in Western cultures since the Industrial Revolution, it has been taken for granted that productive work must be a burden of survival, whether one likes it or not. School learning, like work, is expected to be a generally negative experience for both students and teachers. Compulsory education (as if education could ever be compulsory) is generally seen as a painful necessity for all concerned. When workers report their experiences from work, and students from school, it is clear that the motivations that keep them at their task are rarely intrinsic (Csikszentmihalyi, Larson, and Prescott, 1977; Csikszentmihalyi and Graef, 1980).

In the nineteenth century, when factory operatives worked fourteen and more hours a day, six days a week, with a forty-five minute break for dinner (Thompson, 1963; Wallace, 1978), few people questioned what the workers were actually getting out of life. The goal of workers was to serve the needs of production. Productivity justified their existence and assured their eternal salvation. How workers felt while accomplishing this was entirely irrelevant.

By now most people accept as common sense the fact that work has to be boring or exhausting. It is seen as a means to obtain a financial reward that then can be used, in the worker's free time, to achieve the real goals that justify existence. Intrinsic rewards are not expected from work itself. This view has almost achieved the status of an inevitable law of nature. Yet there is evidence to suggest that making a living need not conflict with a person's well-being.

A few surviving societies based on hunting and gathering give us a glimpse of productive systems that do not require adults to spend their lives doing things they would rather not be doing. As Sahlins (1972), Turnbull (1962), and others have shown, work in pre-agrarian cultures was not only much less demanding than it later became—on the order of three to five hours a day—but it was also considerably freer, more challenging, and enjoyable. Work was not distinguished from the rest of life—not an undesirable means to a desirable end, but integrated such that one could not tell work apart from socializing, performance, worship, or from simply having fun.

The rationalization of production techniques in industrial societies has isolated work from most other meaningful experiences. The ideal or typical assembly-line worker operates in a restricted environment; attention must be concentrated on a strictly limited stimulus field that allows only the most routine forms of human experience to occur. The same pattern of operating efficiency has spread to other jobs, whether clerical, bureaucratic, or technical. With the advent of operant system designs, this pattern threatens to shackle even the liberal profession of university teaching. We have grown accustomed to think that work is something to be tolerated in order to achieve future goals and leisure, even though in itself work may be a fundamentally alienating experience. Industrial psychologists have given their blessing to this state of affairs, advising, as it were, workers to resign themselves to their meaningless jobs for the sake of the paycheck at the end of the week. By and large, this is also the attitude taken by most unions.

Like the king's invisible clothes, the irrationality of this view is rarely questioned. What is the purpose of producing more, of saving, of accumulating material resources, if one's productive activity is, from the worker's point of view, wasted? If work is not enjoyable, if it does not allow a sense of growth and freedom, what makes one suppose that the rest of life will be enjoyable, free, and growth-producing? Not only does the job take up a substantial amount of time and energy (and become, therefore, quantitatively a large part of one's life); it is also a qualitatively unique aspect of life. As Marx argued in his early manuscripts (Tucker, 1978), productive work provides essential feedback to the human self that cannot be obtained from any other source. Acquiescing to the alienation of work means giving up the possibility of developing an integrated self.

Intrinsic Motivation and Higher Education Process

In human terms, any act that is not intrinsically motivating is wasteful. An activity is intrinsically motivated when the actor experiences it as rewarding in itself, not just as a means to future, external goals. Life is wasted to the extent that it is spent doing things that one does not wish to do. These considerations, which apply to work in general, have a particular relevance to higher education. The point is that for a professor, intrinsic motivation is both the product of the activity and the means by which the product is realized.

Basically, teaching involves changing the learners' cognitive structures, and, more importantly, changing their goal structures. The product of teaching is a socialized individual, a young person who shares the goals valued in a given society. At the university level, this socialization includes a set of intellectual goals. To accomplish this end, the teacher is supposed to transmit information and award rewards and punishments (or positive and negative feedback), contingent on the learner's progress (or, rather, this is the operant model on which teaching machines are based).

Actually, transmission of information is of marginal importance to the primary goals of teaching. In this respect, Carl Rogers was right when he said: "It seems to me that anything that can be taught to another is relatively inconsequential and has little or no significant influence on behavior. . . . I have come to feel that the only learning which significantly influences behavior is self-discovered, self-appropriated learning. Such self-discovered learning, truth that has been personally appropriated and assimilated in experience, cannot be directly communicated to another" (Marty, 1979, pp. 196–197).

Although it is true that information is transmitted in lectures and seminars, the real task of a professor is to enable the learner to enjoy learning. Education works when the student becomes intrinsically motivated to acquire the information or the goals to be transmitted; at that point, the major part of the teacher's task is accomplished. Learning motivated by extrinsic rewards is costly to maintain and easy to extinguish in the absence of reward contingencies. Recent experimental evidence suggests that, contrary to behaviorist assumptions, extrinsic rewards might in some circumstances inhibit rather than promote learning (Lepper and Greene, 1978; see also the chapters by Deci and Ryan; McKeachie; and Hall and Bazerman in this volume).

The product of teaching, then, is an intrinsically motivated learner. A teacher has done his or her job when the students enjoy learning and look upon the activity of learning as an end in itself, rather than as a means to an external goal—a grade, a diploma, or a job. Admittedly, it is difficult to measure teaching effectiveness by this criterion. It is easier to measure it by the amount of information transmitted to the student, but such a criterion is not terribly useful unless one knows whether the students want to retain, use, and increase the information learned. Knowledge that is not intrinsically motivated is not much good to anybody.

Intrinsic Motivation and the Students

If the product of teaching is a student who enjoys learning, what are the means by which a teacher can accomplish this purpose? How does one get students to enjoy learning? Here, again, the answer is in principle very simple: by enjoying learning. A teacher who is intrinsically motivated to learn has a good chance to get students to seek the intrinsic rewards of learning.

Young people are more intelligent than adults generally give them credit for. They can usually discern, for instance, whether an adult they know likes or dislikes what he or she is doing. If a teacher does not believe in his job, does not enjoy the learning he is trying to transmit, the student will sense this and derive the entirely rational conclusion that the particular subject matter is not worth mastering for its own sake. If all the teachers they are exposed to are extrinsically motivated, they might well conclude that learning in general is worthless in and of itself.

Such a reaction on the part of young people is eminently adaptive. Why should they want to spend their lives being bored? Why should they emulate a model who is already alienated from his or her life activity? The young are in general less resigned than adults to the prospect of a meaningless life. They look around them for adults who seem to enjoy their jobs, who believe in what they are doing, and take them as models. Of course, young people can also be fooled, like everyone else. They get fooled by people whose job is to pretend to enjoy what they are doing — that is, professional athletes and entertainers who try to convince the uncommitted youth that it is worth growing up because adult life can be enjoyable (Csikszentmihalyi, 1981).

In close quarters it is more difficult to dupe a young person into believing that something matters when it does not. Professors who are cynical about their jobs, who do not enjoy what they are doing, do not help the transmission of knowledge; they only spread cynicism down another generation. At the same time, a teacher who loves the subject, who enjoys the process of thinking, is the most convincing argument for the usefulness of knowledge. This does not mean, of course, that if Ms. X enjoys mathematics, all of her students will adopt her for a model and become intrinsically motivated to pursue mathematics. Too many other variables help to determine the process: the students' talents, competing interests, the degree to which they are already convinced that math is boring or meaningless. But even those students who will never be turned on to math will know that it is indeed possible to love it, because Ms. X bore witness to that unlikely possibility. And that knowledge might in the long run be more useful than facility in calculus.

When students are asked about teachers who were influential in their lives, and the reasons for such influence, their answers do not fit into the theories that social scientists have developed to account for the effectiveness of role modeling. According to current theories, a young person wants to imitate an adult who has status and power, someone who has control over desired resources, who can reward and punish (Bandura and Walters, 1963; Bronfenbrenner, 1973). Socialization is supposed to be based primarily on fear, envy, and greed. Somehow this neat explanation manages to ignore the rather obvious fact that young people (and not only they, as the increasing incidence of mid-life crises shows) will imitate adults who find life worth living, even in the absence of status, power, and control over resources.

The most influential teachers — those who are remembered, who made a difference in the way we see ourselves and the world, who stirred us in new directions, and who revealed unexpected strengths in us or made us aware of our limitations—are not necessarily the ones who had more status, power, or control. They might or might not be exceptionally intelligent or knowledgeable, but they *are* usually the ones who love what they are doing, who show by their dedication and their passion that there is nothing else on earth they would rather be doing.

Students often describe their most influential teacher with some variation of: "Oh, he was such a nut!" Not, as it turns out, because the teacher was funny or entertaining, but simply because his or her involvement in the subject matter seemed, by normal standards, to be excessive—in fact, almost crazy. Yet it is such holy fools who keep the fabric of knowledge from unraveling between one generation and the next. If it weren't for them, who would believe that knowledge really mattered?

It is the teacher who cares about his or her craft who makes students want to care for theirs. As I was writing these pages, one of the teachers I had had in college died. At his funeral, I was trying to figure out how he had managed to make such a difference in my life and in the lives of several other former students who had come to mourn his passing. Robert Nickle, who taught design at the University of Illinois for several decades, was a terrible teacher. He could not explain what he wanted from us, nor did he try to; he did not demonstrate how to do things; his feedback to students was erratic and arbitrary. We were in a constant state of uncertainty and confusion in his classes. He violated all the rules of rational transmission of information; he was the exact antithesis of a well-designed teaching machine. Yet what a great professor he was! His concern for good design, for the integrity of vision and execution, was clear to everybody; it was etched in the lines of pain on his face when confronted with a facile drawing, or in the look of exultation that—alas, much more rarely—passed over his features when someone broke away from a conventional cliché. It was clear that he enjoyed every minute of his work, even though most of it was painful. He could not fake enthusiasm, conviction, or belief either for our sake or for his own, but this very submission to the rules of art generated enthusiasm, conviction, and belief on our parts.

If I think back on the other teachers since college who have had similar effects on me—and how few they were—the same characteristics emerge. Whether the subject matter was philosophy, or statistics, or psychology, it is not the knowledge or prestige of teachers that I remember, or the correctness of their methods. It is, rather, the conviction they conveyed that what they were doing was worth doing, that it was intrinsically valuable. This is the means by which the goal of education can be achieved, and it is not something teaching machines or audio-visual aids can be built to simulate. It is not the transmission of information, but the transmission of meaning that is involved (Nehari and Bender, 1978). Information can be conveyed in many ways: books, instruments, machines, and so forth. Meaning, which refers to information that is integrated in terms of a person's life goals, cannot be taught; it can only be demonstrated in one's own actions. This is essentially the kind of learning Carl Rogers, in the quote above, has called "self-discovered." A person who professes a set of meanings has a chance to stimulate such discovery — or the meaningful integration of information — in others.

On the most general level, education refers to the process by which youths agree to become adults. It is not just a question of behaving like adults, but of *liking to be* adults. That this process is not an automatic one is shown by the 300 percent increase in adolescent suicides over the past thirty years *(Social Indicators,* 1981; Wynne, 1978), and by the similar increases in drug addiction, delinquency, and other forms of deviance. These trends indicate that young persons in our society are refusing, in increasing numbers, to grow up into adulthood. Education fails when becoming an adult is no longer a desirable option.

From this point of view, the main function of the teacher is not to teach science, math, or literature; it is to make being an adult seem like a worthwhile option. Of course, this modeling responsibility is not peculiar to teachers alone, but rests upon every adult member of our society. The task specific to teachers is to demonstrate, by their own example, that being an *educated* adult is a goal worth striving for.

It is possible that the survival of a culture over time depends on whether the older generations are able to convince the younger ones that growing up makes sense. To be convinced, a youth has to feel that being an adult can be meaningful. This in turn requires exposure to persons who derive intrinsic rewards from adult roles. Similarly, young people will not want to become philosophers or scientists if their teachers do not enjoy philosophy or science. Even within a given field, the development of subfields seems to be a function of differential intrinsic rewards. As Kuhn (1970) suggests, young scholars will move to research areas that promise to be exciting and enjoyable, and abandon those that seem boring. Thus, intrinsic motivation is a crucial link in the transmission of cultural forms across time.

A Basis of Enjoyable — Motivated — Teaching

The argument thus far has tried to establish two points: that lack of enjoyment in teaching deprives the activity of its main value for both the teacher and the student. The teacher who does not find his or her subject matter worthwhile in and of itself, but teaches it only for extrinsic reasons — pay or prestige — wastes his own time and conveys the message to students that learning is only a means to other ends and lacks intrinsic value.

The question then becomes "What makes teaching enjoyable?" Is it possible to learn to enjoy teaching? While one can certainly learn to enjoy teaching, I have shown that learning cannot be taught. The intrinsic rewards and the meaning of the activity must be discovered on one's own. It is possible, however, to reflect on those aspects of teaching that have the greatest potential for providing intrinsic rewards, and to experiment with them until a personally meaningful combination of rewards is discovered. To facilitate this task, we shall review a general model of enjoyment that has been found useful in a variety of contexts, and then apply it to the activity of teaching.

Our research with intrinsically motivated individuals suggests that whenever a person has fun — whether it is dancing or playing chess, climbing a mountain or studying in a classroom — a similar set of inner experiences and environmental conditions is present (Csikszentmihalyi, 1975, 1978a, 1978b, 1979; Csikszentmihalyi and Larson, 1978; Mayers, Csikszentmihalyi, and Larson, 1978). The experience of enjoyment — or flow, as we came to call it — is characterized above all by a deep, spontaneous involvement with the task at hand. In flow, one is carried away by interaction to the extent that one feels immersed in the activity — the distinction between "I" and "it" becomes irrelevant. Attention is focused on whatever needs to be done, and there is not enough left to worry or to get bored and distracted. In a state of flow, a person knows what needs to be done and whether the goals are being achieved or not — the feedback is clear. Yet the question of whether one is doing well or not seems to matter little; in flow, a person does not worry about his or her performance. The sense of time becomes distorted; hours seem to pass by in minutes, but afterward one might feel that an eternity has elapsed. The ego that surveys and evaluates our actions disappears in the flow of experience. One is freed of the confines of the social self and may feel an exhilarating sense of transcendence, of belonging to a larger whole.

These qualities describe how people feel when they enjoy what they are doing. Surgeons in the operating room or laborers on the assembly line use the same words to describe their work when it is enjoyable and rewarding. What we know about flow is that its presence depends a great deal on two conditions: how the activity is structured objectively, and how the person perceives the structure of the activity. For instance, every game is structured so as to make the focusing of attention on the play activity easy, and it provides clear goals, rules, and feedback. These structural features engage the player's attention, producing a flow experience. However, a person might restructure stimuli in his or her consciousness so as to produce flow without assistance from pre-structured patterns in the environment and thus experience flow outside of ready-made cultural play forms. This is what children, yogis, mathematicians, artists, and countless unsung average people can do at times.

A decisive structural factor for enjoyment is the balance of challenges and skills. At any given moment, we process in consciousness two crucial pieces of information: "What can be done here?" and "What am I capable of?" The first question deals with the opportunities for action in the environment, or challenges. The second concerns one's own capacity to act, or skills. When challenges overwhelm skills, we feel anxious; when skills outweigh challenges, we feel bored. Flow occurs when we come close to matching the two. Here, again, we meet the external and internal dialectic of flow: challenges and skills are partly objective features of the situation; partly they are the results of one's subjective attitude. The two are related, and both are important in producing the experience.

An essential feature of this structure of challenges and skills is that their balance is not static. If the complexity of challenges one faces does not increase with time, flow gives way to boredom. As we practice an activity, our skills in it increase until they outweigh the challenges. Hence, to maintain flow, there must be provisions made to find new things to engage our attention and skill, lest what used to be fun drift into tedium.

In summary, any activity can become rewarding if it provides the following requirements:

1. The activity should be structured so that the actor can increase or decrease the level of challenges being faced in order to match exactly his or her skills with the requirements for action.

2. It should be easy to isolate the activity at least at the perceptual level from other stimuli — external or internal — that might interfere with involvement in it.

3. There should be clear criteria for performance; one should be able to evaluate how well or poorly one is doing at any time.

4. The activity should provide concrete feedback to the actor so that one can tell how well one is meeting the criteria of performance.

5. The activity ought to have a broad range of challenges — possibly several qualitatively different ranges of challenge — so that the actor may obtain increasingly complex information about different aspects of the self [Csikszentmihalyi, 1978b].

Establishing Flow in Teaching

In teaching, two main action systems provide intrinsic rewards. One is the educational process itself (that is, the changes in the student's performance attributable to the teacher's actions). The challenges here are to attract and maintain the students' attention, and to motivate them to pursue goals valued by the teacher. The second set of intrinsic rewards is provided by the subject matter. The challenges here refer to the continuing integration of new information on the teacher's part. In other words, it is the teacher's own learning that is enjoyable. Although these two aspects are independent of each other — one can enjoy teaching without learning much that is new about the subject matter, and vice versa — they are not mutually exclusive. In fact, teaching is probably most effective when the teacher enjoys both processes at the same time.

Subject Matter. Presumably there are subject matter differences in the ease of establishing flow in a classroom. Science and math, for instance, have the initial disadvantage of presenting too many challenges to students, who start out being anxious and often remain in that state without ever enjoying the learning process. But once skills are matched to challenges, it is probably easier to sustain the flow experience in science and math than in humanities or social sciences, because the goals, the rules, and the feedback are much less ambiguous in the former. Certain subjects, such as art, music, or drama, have the advantage of clearly demarcating the field from everyday life, and therefore admitting greater concentration with fewer distractions.

Classroom Structure. Structural aspects of the classroom situation will also have an effect on how much enjoyment teaching affords. For instance, lecturing to a large class makes it almost impossible for the teacher to monitor individual changes in students. Similarly, if students are seen for only a semester or a year, feedback about their changes to the teacher will be meager. Without such feedback, there is little enjoyment to be derived at the educational level. A class that consists of students with widely different levels of preparation also detracts from the enjoyment of teaching because the challenges facing the teacher are incongruent with each other. A structurally adversary relationship between teacher and students, as in required courses, also has the same effects. If for these or other reasons teaching cannot be turned into a flow activity, the effectiveness of the class will be reduced for both teacher and students because the experience will cease to be intrinsically rewarding.

In conditions that make teaching unrewarding, the professor may change the rules and shift into a performing mode. As a performer, he or she need not be concerned with specific changes in individual students; the feedback that counts is the audience's spellbound attention. Charismatic teachers—those who have the skills to project meanings—might enjoy classroom conditions that would make others bored or anxious. Such teaching is effective insofar as it communicates to the students that the teacher values knowledge for its own sake, and therefore enjoys the symbolic manipulation of knowledge. Of course, other things might be communicated as well, messages that conflict with the educational goal; for instance, that the teacher enjoys being the center of attention, that his rewards derive from being powerful or entertaining.

It falls outside the scope of this chapter to detail techniques that might turn teaching into a flow activity. Research could help identify and describe such techniques, but at this point there are virtually no studies of intrinsic motivation in teaching. Some of the chapters in this volume, particularly those by Deci and Ryan, McKeachie, Cammann, and Mowday, suggest techniques that are congruent with the flow model either by demonstrating how distractions can be eliminated, or how conditions for involvement with challenges can be enhanced. General studies of teachers—like the ones by Lortie (1975); Dubin and Champoux (1977); and Miskel, de Frain, and Wilcox (1980)—have started to explore the motivational structure of educators, but their perspective is still too broad to provide the kind of detail needed to know how teaching is to be turned into an enjoyable experience. Apparently there is no study relating the teacher's motivation to the effectiveness of his or her teaching—in other words, to the students' motivation. One pilot study by Plihal (1981) shows that grade school students pay more attention in the classes of teachers who rate enjoyment as the highest reward of teaching. Obviously, we need more studies of this type at higher levels of education.

In fact, a great many questions arise if one accepts as testable the propositions advanced here. To accept them, one must modify current assumptions about the effectiveness of teaching. Instead of emphasizing transmission of information as the criterion of good teaching, the importance of intrinsic motivation, both as a means and as a goal of education, should be recognized.

References

Bandura, A., and Walters, R. H. *Social Learning and Personality Development.* New York: Holt, Rinehart, and Winston, 1963.

Bronfenbrenner, U. *Two Worlds of Childhood.* New York: Pocket Books, 1973.

Csikszentmihalyi, M. *Beyond Boredom and Anxiety.* San Francisco: Jossey-Bass, 1975.

Csikszentmihalyi, M. "Attention and the Wholistic Approach to Behavior." In K. S. Pope and J. L. Singer (Eds.), *The Stream of Consciousness.* New York: Plenum, 1978a.

Csikszentmihalyi, M. "Intrinsic Rewards and Emergent Motivation." In M. R. Lepper and D. Greene (Eds.), *The Hidden Costs of Reward.* New York: Erlbaum, 1978b.

Csikszentmihalyi, M. "The Concept of Flow." In B. Sutton-Smith (Ed.), *Play and Learning.* New York: Gardner, 1979.

Csikszentmihalyi, M. "Leisure and Socialization." *Social Forces,* 1981, *60* (2), 332–340.

Csikszentmihalyi, M., and Graef, R. "The Experience of Freedom in Daily Life." *American Journal of Community Psychology,* 1980, *8* (4), 401–414.

Csikszentmihalyi, M., and Larson, R. "Intrinsic Rewards in School Crime." *Crime and Delinquency,* 1978, *24* (3), 322–335.

Csikszentmihalyi, M., Larson, R., and Prescott, S. "The Ecology of Adolescent Activity and Experience." *Journal of Youth and Adolescence,* 1977, *6* (3), 281–294.

Dubin, R., and Champoux, J. "Central Life Interests and Job Satisfaction." *Organic Behavior and Human Performance,* 1977, *18,* 366–377.

Kuhn, T. S. *The Structure of Scientific Revolutions.* Chicago: The University of Chicago Press, 1970.

Lepper, M. R., and Greene, D. (Eds.). *The Hidden Costs of Reward.* New York: Erlbaum, 1978.

Lortie, D. C. *Schoolteacher.* Chicago: University of Chicago Press, 1975.

Marty, M. A. "Teaching History Today." *Theology Today,* 1979, *36* (2), 195–199.

Mayers, P. L., Csikszentmihalyi, M., and Larson, R. "The Daily Experience of High School Students." Presented at the American Educational Research Association annual meetings, Toronto, 1978.

Miskel, C., de Frain, J. A., and Wilcox, K. "A Test of Expectancy Work Motivation Theory in Educational Organizations." *Educational Administration Quarterly,* 1980, *16* (1), 70–92.

Nehari, M., and Bender, H. "Meaningfulness of a Learning Experience: A Measure for Educational Outcomes in Higher Education." *Higher Education,* 1978, *7,* 1–11.

Plihal, J. "Intrinsic Rewards of Teaching." Paper presented at the American Educational Research Assocation meetings, Los Angeles, 1981.

Sahlins, M. *Stone Age Economics.* Chicago: Aldine, 1972.

Social Indicators, III. Washington, D.C.: Department of Commerce, 1981.

Thompson, E. P. *The Making of the English Working Class.* New York: Vintage, 1963.

Tucker, R. C. *The Marx-Engels Reader.* New York: Norton, 1978.

Turnbull, C. M. *The Forest People.* New York: Simon and Schuster, 1962.

26

Wallace, A. F. C. *Rockdale*. New York: Knopf, 1978.
Wynne, E. A. "Behind the Discipline Problem: Youth Suicide as a Measure of Alienation." *Phi Delta Kappan*, 1978, *59* (5), 397–315.

*Mihalyi Csikszentmihalyi is professor of behavioral sciences and education
and chairman of the Committee on Human Development at the University
of Chicago.*

Teaching can be intrinsically motivating by providing opportunities for competent and self-determined activity, if rewards and structures are administered wisely.

Intrinsic Motivation to Teach: Possibilities and Obstacles in Our Colleges and Universities

Edward L. Deci
Richard M. Ryan

Discussions of motivation and education typically focus on motivating students to learn. Insofar as teachers are mentioned, it is generally in terms of what they should do to motivate and improve the performance of the students in their courses. Our own research has been of this type, and our discussions have focused largely on how teachers' orientations toward control versus autonomy have an impact on students' motivation.

Recently we conducted a training program for teachers in which the aim was to foster more autonomy orientation among teachers since previous research had indicated that children in the classes of autonomy-oriented teachers were more intrinsically motivated. The most interesting result of the program was our realization that the principles which we had derived from our research on students' motivation to learn turned out to be equally relevant for teachers' motivation to teach.

Preparation of this chapter was facilitated by Research Grant BSN-8018628 from the National Science Foundation to the first author. Opinions, findings, and conclusions or recommendations expressed here are those of the authors and do not necessarily reflect the views of the National Science Foundation.

J. Bess (Ed.). *New Directions for Teaching and Learning: Motivating Professors to Teach Effectively*, no. 10. San Francisco: Jossey-Bass, June 1982.

27

Intrinsic and Extrinsic Motivation

We begin with the assumption that people are intrinsically motivated to learn; they are curious and eager to try new things. This is most apparent among young children for whom learning is the main business of life, but it is true for adults as well. Frequently one hears adults express a longing for relaxed time to read or learn a new skill. They seem to desire these opportunities because they enjoy learning and knowing; it is intrinsically interesting to discover and understand new things. Intrinsic motivation is based on the innate need to be competent and self-determining (White, 1959; deCharms, 1968; Deci, 1975). This basic need leads people to situations and activities that interest them, that provide optimal challenges, that allow them to learn and achieve.

In spite of this innate curiosity, however, various characteristics of the environment affect people's motivation to learn and perform. A wealth of research studies has enumerated the conditions within which intrinsic motivation is likely to be diminished and enhanced (see Deci and Ryan, 1980, for an extensive review). In essence, experiences that leave people feeling less self-determining and less competent will undermine their intrinsic motivation, while experiences that leave people feeling more self-determining and more competent will bolster their intrinsic motivation.

Research has shown that monetary rewards (Deci, 1971), good player awards (Lepper, Greene, and Nisbett, 1973), food rewards (Ross, 1975), threats of punishment (Deci and Cascio, 1972), surveillance (Lepper and Greene, 1975), explicit competition (Deci and others, 1981), and external evaluation of performance (Smith, 1974) can all decrease intrinsic motivation. Cognitive evaluation theory (Deci and Ryan, 1980) holds that these experiences induce a change in perceived locus of causality from internal to external and leave people feeling less self-determining. Whereas doing an activity out of interest and curiosity has an internal locus of causality, doing it to get a reward or comply with a constraint shifts the locus of causality to the external reward. The activity becomes instrumental and is no longer engaged in for its own sake.

On the other hand, when subjects are given a choice about various aspects of the task they are doing, they are more intrinsically motivated (Zuckerman and others, 1978). We suggest that the choice—the opportunity to be self-determining—produces a shift in perceived locus of causality toward greater internality. In sum, one process by which external factors can affect intrinsic motivation is a change in perceived locus of causality. If the perceived causality becomes more external, intrinsic motivation will have decreased; if it becomes more internal, intrinsic motivation will have increased.

Other studies have shown that success and positive feedback lead to greater intrinsic motivation (Anderson, Manoogian, and Reznick, 1976; Blanck, Jackson, and Reis, 1979); whereas failure and negative feedback lead to decreased intrinsic motivation (Deci, Cascio, and Krusell, 1973). Cognitive evaluation theory holds that the second process through which intrinsic motivation can be affected is a change in perceived competence. Success experiences and positive feedback increase people's perceived competence at an activity, thereby increasing their intrinsic motivation. Failure experiences and negative feedback decrease perceived competence, thereby decreasing intrinsic motivation.

Although research has tended to show that rewards decrease intrinsic motivation by co-opting people's self-determination, it is perfectly plausible to conjecture that rewards might increase intrinsic motivation by signifying competence. Indeed, we have suggested (Deci and Ryan, 1980) that rewards and communications have both a controlling and an informational component. Thus, we hypothesized that if a reward is administered in a controlling way it will decrease intrinsic motivation, whereas if it is administered in a way that conveys competence at a chosen activity, the reward should increase intrinsic motivation. This hypothesis has been supported in recent studies by Enzle and Ross (1978), Pittman and others (1980), Rosenfield, Folger, and Adelman (1980), and Ryan (1981).

Teachers' Orientations; Students' Motivations

On the basis of the experimental findings described above, we concluded that students will be more intrinsically motivated to learn if their environments provide them with (1) the opportunity to be self-determining and (2) activities that are optimally challenging so that concerted efforts can lead to eventual success. We reasoned that teachers who are oriented toward supporting autonomy will tend to create such an environment, whereas teachers who are oriented toward controlling their students will tend not to provide such an environment. We (Deci, Nezlek, and Sheinman, 1981; Deci and others, in press) tested this in public schools, although the results seem to be generalizable to colleges as well. We measured the orientations of thirty-five teachers as well as the intrinsic motivation of the children in their classrooms. We found a strong correlation between the two; teachers who are autonomy-oriented had children who were more intrinsically motivated, while teachers who were control-oriented had children who were less intrinsically motivated. Further, the children in the autonomy-oriented classrooms had higher self-esteem than the children in the control-oriented classrooms.

The research was done in traditional suburban schools. The autonomy-oriented teachers, like the control-oriented teachers, used rewards, grades, and constraints of various sorts. However, we infer that the autonomy-oriented teachers tended to use rewards and constraints more *informationally*, whereas control-oriented teachers tended to use them more *controllingly*.

From our own experiences of teaching in universities, the same conclusion seems warranted. When teachers tend to be controlling, the students either comply resentfully or react defiantly. Regardless of which strategy the students adopt, the experiences tend to undermine their intrinsic motivation and impair their learning.

People are quick to point out that some students seem to ask for controlling structures; they seem to want to be told what to do and how to do it. This, we suggest, results from their having been controlled and having adopted the compliant strategy. For teachers to perpetuate this type of response in the students by being controlling may, however, be doing a disservice to the students, for it is not helping them become more self-reliant and intrinsically motivated.

Motivation for Teaching

Our basic assumption about motivation for teaching, like our basic assumption about motivation for learning, is that most teachers are (or at least start out being) highly intrinsically motivated to teach. Teaching offers the opportunity to have a meaningful effect on students, and although the real impact that one's teaching can have may take years to be realized, one can still see immediate effects as students respond and become excited about new ideas. In one study, Benware and Deci (1981) found that when subjects learn material with the expectation of teaching it to other people, they report being more intrinsically motivated to learn the material than other subjects who learned the material in order to be tested on it. We understand this finding in terms of the subjects' seeing teaching as a place in which they can have an important impact on their environment; they were interested in learning the material because they would be able to use it in the intrinsically motivating activity of teaching.

Not only does teaching allow one the opportunity to have an effect on one's environment, it typically allows considerable freedom to teach in one's own way. There is less surveillance and direct evaluation than in many other jobs. This is particularly true at the college level, since professors are free to teach the courses they want, to cover the material that interests them, and to use the methods of teaching that suit them best. In universities, of course, the issue is somewhat complicated, since teaching is not necessarily the central element of the job; university professors are frequently hired to be scholars and scientists rather than teachers. Still, from our experience, we have found that most professors enjoy teaching very much — except when they are feeling pressured. They are intrinsically motivated to communicate to others the ideas that interest them, and they are especially eager to talk about their own work. The challenge of getting students "turned on" to new ideas can be tremendously exciting and rewarding. Thus, it appears that, even for college teachers, the problem is not so much one of motivating them to teach as it is one of not undermining the motivation that they have. As with motivating students to learn, it is a matter of providing the conditions within which teachers' intrinsic motivation can flourish.

Positive and Negative Factors of Motivation

Just as students, who by nature are intrinsically motivated to learn, often display signs of being unmotivated, teachers, who begin with considerable intrinsic motivation to teach, also display signs of being unmotivated. One need only listen to experienced professors to discover how their creativity and vitality for teaching has too often been dissipated. Various conditions have turned their excitement into frustration, their creativity into cynicism. Let us therefore consider the conditions that deplete teachers' intrinsic motivation as well as those that facilitate or replenish it.

The research mentioned earlier is directly applicable to this problem. Just as rewards, deadlines, constraints, surveillance, and external evaluations tend to undermine students' intrinsic motivation to learn, so do they undermine teachers' intrinsic motivation to teach. Just as students, in order to remain motivated to learn, need teachers who respond to their initiations and support their attempts to be self-competent, in the same way teachers, in order to remain intrinsically motivated to teach, need administrators and colleagues who respond to and support their similar initiations and attempts. When administrators and colleagues are more autonomy-oriented, when teachers have opportunities to try new things, to teach in idiosyncratic ways, to choose optimal challenges, they seem to be more intrinsically motivated. When the organizational climate is oriented toward supporting autonomy and providing challenges, motivating teachers is unlikely to be a problem.

Unfortunately, the conditions that facilitate intrinsic motivation for teachers may be more the exception than the rule. Our experiences as teachers and our interviews with other teachers have suggested that there are many threats to the fulfillment of intrinsic needs.

Shrinking Resources; Growing Pressures. In colleges and universities, resources seem to be shrinking. There are fewer college-age people than there were five years ago, yet there are more people with doctorates than ever before. There are more people to do the teaching, but fewer people to be taught. Federal funding is also shrinking, and still further cuts in support for education and basic research have been promised for the near future.

All of this may have a direct impact on teachers' feelings of self-determination and competence. First, the pressure to produce is greater than ever. People completing their doctorates need several publications to be considered for university faculty positions; promotions not only require significantly more publications than was the case a decade ago, but it is becoming increasingly important that people obtain their own research funding in order to be promoted or tenured.

As Mann and others (1970) pointed out, the teaching culture has an important impact on teachers. The ambience created by a group of colleagues affects each member of the group. As resources shrink, people tend to be more competitive, more self-concerned, and the ambience becomes less supportive.

Further, the realities of shrinking resources cause difficult problems for administrators, which often result in their being more controlling, creating still further pressures for faculty members.

That is not intended as a criticism of administrators; the point is that the pressures they feel, like the pressures both students and teachers feel, leave them less intrinsically motivated. All the research mentioned earlier indicates that these extrinsic pressures — the deadlines, evaluations, and other controls — will shift the perceived locus of causality toward the external elements and undermine intrinsic motivation.

Feelings of competence are also vulnerable to these changing conditions, especially in domains where the standards for evaluation have risen. Getting grants, for example, is seen as very important — even for junior faculty members who were never before expected to get grants — at the same time that grant agencies have less money to give. Is it any wonder that faculty members will feel less competent, less able to have an impact on their environment?

In terms of teaching, these pressures can have serious consequences. Growing external pressures can have three potential effects on faculty members' intrinsic motivation to teach. First, the pressure tends to make the perceived locus of causality for *all* of their professional activities more external, such that teachers are likely to be less intrinsically motivated for *all* aspects of their professional roles. People simply do not maintain an intrinsic orientation when they feel pressured. Second, since evaluations are based largely on scholarly output, little importance is given to teaching. People tend not to use teaching as a realm in which to direct their mastery attempts, and as they spend less time on teaching, they are likely to teach less well and to feel less competent as teachers.

Finally, the increased pressure seems to be resulting in a higher degree of failure for faculty members; fewer people are making it through the stringent evaluations. The feelings of incompetence that result from not being reappointed or promoted, from not publishing and doing research that works out, are likely to generalize to their feelings about teaching. The result will be low self-esteem and a minimum of intrinsic motivation.

The goal of most educators to develop intrinsically motivated students seems best achieved by having intrinsically motivated teachers, by having teachers who are excited, involved, self-directed, and trying new things. When teachers are intrinsically motivated, they will be more supportive of students' independence and mastery. Students need supportive teachers, teachers who are concerned about teaching and oriented toward autonomy. But teachers are unlikely to encourage intrinsic learning since teaching itself is not highly valued and faculty members are being greatly pressured in other areas of their professional activity.

It is ironic that administrators, who appropriately aim to achieve high-quality education, often respond to the difficult realities of academia by creating controls and pressures that deplete teachers' intrinsic motivation and thereby decrease the quality of education.

An Alternative

Of course, the alternative to overcontrol is not an abandonment of structure; that would only create more chaos and anxiety for teachers and students alike. Structures are necessary for people to have a direction and a basis for assessing their own competence. In terms of teaching, this means valuing the activity of teaching and then creating structures that focus on outcomes rather than means, that are informative rather than controlling. The people who live and work within the structures need to have more say in the creation or modification of those structures, and the assessment of performance—the measuring of a teacher against the structure—needs to be more self-directed.

The essence of the alternative is active teaching and active learning, rather than passive teaching and passive learning (Rogers, 1969). By active teaching, we do not mean that the teacher does a lot of lecturing or a lot of controlling; we mean, rather, that the teacher does a lot of creating, exploring, and experimenting. An active teacher will be a resource person, a guide for students' active learning. In active teaching, as in active learning, the locus of decision for how to teach would rest primarily with the teachers, who, one would hope, could create an environment where self-initiated learning could flourish. Teachers would facilitate learning rather than control and evaluate it. Analogously, administrators in such a system would facilitate involved teaching rather than controlling and evaluating it. We suggest that when teachers are supported and valued for trying new things, for succeeding and for failing, their teaching will be more active. In turn, they will be more likely to provide the setting within which the students will be able to explore, to create, to try, and to err.

Teachers would be held responsible for their teaching and students would be held responsible for their learning, but the ambience within which they would be held responsible would be an ambience of freedom and flexibility, an ambience of support and trust. The idea of responsibility is, of course, tricky, for it tends to foster surveillance and evaluation, both of which have been shown to undermine intrinsic motivation. The goal is to instill and support a self-responsibility in which teachers would be doing well out of their own desire to be competent. To do this, administrators need to provide positive feedback for work well done, they need to involve faculty members in goal setting and self-evaluation, to display the type of supportive attitude that encourages teachers to want to teach well, and to set an example of high-quality, self-directed, responsible, and relaxed performance of their own functions.

Conditions Create Motivated Teaching

Teaching, like learning, is an intrinsically motivating activity. Teachers seem to enjoy teaching and they seem to begin their careers with enthusiasm. Motivating them is not a problem. But when their teaching is controlled, when they feel pressured, hurried, and evaluated in their teaching, they gradually lose their intrinsic motivation to teach, just as students lose their intrinsic motivation to learn when their learning is controlled, pressured, and evaluated.

Times are becoming more difficult in colleges and universities, and the pressure appears to be building. Thus, it is increasingly imperative that administrators work to create the conditions that promote rather than drain intrinsic motivation. The keys to creating these conditions seem to be administrators' orientations toward autonomy and structures that inform rather than control. If conditions are created that bolster teachers' feelings of competence and self-determination, teachers' motivation to teach will take care of itself.

References

Amabile, T. M., DeJong, W., and Lepper, M. R. "Effects of Externally Imposed Deadlines on Subsequent Intrinsic Motivation." *Journal of Personality and Social Psychology,* 1976, *34,* 92–98.

Anderson, R., Manoogian, S. T., and Reznick, J. S. "The Undermining and Enhancing of Intrinsic Motivation in Pre-School Children." *Journal of Personality and Social Psychology,* 1976, *34,* 915–922.

Benware, C., and Deci, E. L. "The Quality of Learning with an Active Versus Passive Motivational Set." Unpublished manuscript, University of Rochester, 1981.

Blanck, P., Jackson, L., and Reis, H. T. "Effects of Verbal Praise on Intrinsic Motivation for Sex-Typed Tasks." Paper presented at the American Psychological Association convention, New York, 1979.

deCharms, R. *Personal Causation: The Internal Affective Determinants of Behavior.* New York: Academic Press, 1968.

Deci, E. L. "Effects of Externally Mediated Rewards on Intrinsic Motivation." *Journal of Personality and Social Psychology,* 1971, *18,* 105–115.

Deci, E. L. *Intrinsic Motivation.* New York: Plenum, 1975.

Deci, E. L., Betley, G. Kahle, J., Abrams, L., and Porac, J. "When Trying to Win: Competition and Intrinsic Motivation." *Personality and Social Psychology Bulletin,* in press.

Deci, E. L., and Cascio, W. F. "Changes in Intrinsic Motivation as A Function of Negative Feedback and Threats." Eastern Psychological Association convention, Boston, 1972.

Deci, E. L., Cascio, W. F., and Krusell, J. "Sex Differences, Positive Feedback and Intrinsic Motivation." Paper presented at the Eastern Psychological Assocation convention, Washington, D.C., 1973.

Deci, E. L., Nezlek, J., and Sheinman, L. "Characteristics of the Rewarder and Intrinsic Motivation of the Rewardee." *Journal of Personality and Social Psychology,* 1981, *40,* 1–10.

Deci, E. L., and Ryan, R. M. "The Empirical Exploration of Intrinsic Motivational Processes." In L. Berkowitz (Ed.), *Advances in Experimental Social Psychology.* Vol. 13. New York: Academic Press, 1980.

Deci, E. L., Schwartz, A. J., Sheinman, L., and Ryan, R. M. "An Instrument to Assess Adults' Orientations Toward Control Versus Autonomy with Children: Reflections on Intrinsic Motivation and Perceived Competence." *Journal of Educational Psychology,* in press.

Enzle, M. E., and Ross, J. M. "Increasing and Decreasing Intrinsic Interest with Contingent Rewards: A Test of Cognitive Evaluation Theory." *Journal of Experimental Social Psychology,* 1978, *14,* 588–597.

Lepper, M. R., and Greene, D. "Turning Play Into Work: Effects of Adult Surveillance and Extrinsic Rewards on Children's Intrinsic Motivation." *Journal of Personality and Social Psychology,* 1975, *31* (3), 479–486.

Lepper, M. R., Greene, D., and Nisbett, R. E. "Undermining Children's Intrinsic Interest with Extrinsic Rewards: A Test of the 'Overjustification' Hypothesis." *Journal of Personality and Social Psychology,* 1973, *28,* 129–137.

Mann, R. D., Arnold, S. M., Binder, J. L., Cytrynbaum, S., Newman, B. M., Ringwald, B. E., and Rosenwein, R. *The College Classroom.* New York: Wiley, 1970.

Pittman, T. S., Davey, M. E., Alafat, K. A., Wetherill, K. V., and Wirsul, N. A. "Informational Versus Controlling Rewards, Levels of Surveillance, and Intrinsic Motivation." *Personality and Social Psychology Bulletin,* 1980, *6,* 228–233.

Rogers, C. *Freedom to Learn.* Columbus, Ohio: Merrill, 1969.

Rosenfield, D., Folger, R., and Adelman, H. "When Rewards Reflect Competence: A Qualification of the Overjustification Effect." *Journal of Personality and Social Psychology,* 1980, *39,* 368–376.

Ross, M. "Salience of Reward and Intrinsic Motivation." *Journal of Personality and Social Psychology,* 1975, *32,* 245–254.

Ryan, R. M. "Self Versus Other Evaluation: An Extension of Cognitive Evaluation Theory to Intrapersonal Processes." Unpublished doctoral dissertation, University of Rochester, 1981.

Smith, W. E. "The Effects of Social and Monetary Rewards on Intrinsic Motivation." Unpublished doctoral dissertation, Cornell University, 1974.

White, R. W. "Motivation Reconsidered: The Concept of Competence." *Psychological Review,* 1959, *66,* 297–333.

Zuckerman, M., Porac, J. F., Lathin, D., Smith, R., and Deci, E. L. "On the Importance of Self-Determination for Intrinsically Motivated Behavior." *Personality and Social Psychology Bulletin,* 1978, *4,* 443–446.

Edward L. Deci is professor of psychology at the University of Rochester.

Richard M. Ryan is assistant professor in the Department of Psychology at the University of Rochester.

Failure to satisfy interpersonal or growth needs
may lead to a preoccupation with material needs.

Human Needs and
Faculty Motivation

Benjamin Schneider
Mary D. Zalesny

People enter occupations and careers for many reasons, including their own abilities and interests as well as the characteristics of the environment in which they grow up and develop. It follows that people who enter academic careers in academic settings probably have a particular subset of abilities, interests, and backgrounds. Further, it can be assumed that success in those careers requires that particular combination of abilities, interests, and background which fits the requirements of those settings. Our purpose in the present chapter is to explore the fit of academic to academe from the vantage point of need theories.

Our operating hypothesis is that there are three basically different kinds of people who may be attracted to academic settings: those who have a desire to teach, those with a desire to do research, and those with an orientation to both teaching and research. Similarly, academic institutions have preferences for, and try to attract, usually one of these types of people. Clearly, this distinction is a simplistic one; career and occupational decisions in academics, as elsewhere, are complex and, to a degree, uniquely individual processes (Bess, 1978). Furthermore, addressing individual needs and motivations would amount to mere speculation. The strength of need theories lies not in their prediction of specific individual behaviors, but rather in their explanation of the motivating force behind human behavior in general. Our purpose,

J. Bess (Ed.). *New Directions for Teaching and Learning: Motivating Professors to Teach Effectively*, no. 10.
San Francisco: Jossey-Bass, June 1982.

then, may be better served by abstracting from the specific and addressing the general needs or preferences that are fulfilled in the academic world. This chapter will focus on an understanding of faculty motivation in colleges and universities, especially in those that prefer faculty members who are oriented to both teaching and research.

Ideally, people find the environments they perfectly fit. This can happen when environmental settings present clear goals and the role of individuals in accomplishing those goals. However, the ideal is rarely achieved in academe. On the one hand, the academic setting conveys some very explicit requirements to be met for continued membership, including tenure; but, on the other hand, the nature of that same setting is to be behaviorally nondirective (no one tells you how to meet those requirements). From this we can conclude that only those people who (1) discover what the requirements of the setting are and (2) match those requirements will be successful.

We begin with the assumption that people who find this kind of setting personally rewarding are likely to enter it and remain in it. What sort of person is this likely to be? We propose that those attracted to and potentially gratified by the relatively unstructured world of academe would be mature individuals with strong self-actualization, growth, and achievement needs, for whom work is as natural as play, and who enjoy a challenge and taking a moderate risk.

There is essentially no direct evidence for our assertion about the kinds of people likely to be successful academics. However, the general literature that does exist on careers suggests that particular kinds of persons can be found in particular kinds of careers and occupations. An important question, of course, is how these people come to be found in those careers. Schein (1978) has summarized two major perspectives that can provide an answer: the differentialist perspective and the developmentalist perspective. In the former, occupations are filled by a matching of a particular person with unique abilities, skills, and interests to a particular occupation. The matching process may be as simple as trial and error carried out by the individuals themselves. It may also be as complex as sophisticated career counseling procedures that assess both person and career attributes.

In the developmentalist view, identity and occupational membership are a part of a continuing sequence of development which begins in childhood and ends in retirement. Occupational membership is the result of long-term consequences of both heredity and early experiences which influence self-image and are, to a large extent, inevitable.

In our view, a person ends up in a career that fits the kind of person he or she has become over time. Thus, this view encompasses both the differentialist and the developmentalist perspectives. Of particular importance, we feel, is the developmentalist's conceptualization of the career "choice" as a natural outcome of identity formation. In contrast, then, to the more rational, cognitive career-choice theories that subscribe to careful calculations by the individual of expectancies and outcomes, the need-theory perspective suggests that the career one enters is a natural consequence of earlier developmental stages. To understand this natural consequence of development, it is important to know what leads people to behave in particular ways, that is, what activates and directs their behavior. Need theories, which are developmental in their perspective, seem to be particularly appropriate as a source of understanding what activates and directs the behavior of the faculty.

Need Theories at Work: The Maslow Heritage

Maslow's (1943, 1954) need-oriented conceptualizations of human motivation are in one way the prototypical need theory: They provide a listing of fundamental wants or desires over which the organism has no control. Maslow, however, not only specifies some of the conditions which might gratify needs, but he also presents a developmental hierarchy of prepotency. This means that (1) lower needs on the hierarchy are assumed to be the first ones encountered in the normal course of development and (2) the higher needs in the hierarchy are activated only after the lower ones are gratified. Maslow's perspective is developmental and deterministic; one *could* move through the hierarchy, but if gratification of a need at a particular stage of development is blocked, one would be stuck there. Mature adults are to be found at the upper need levels, while children and immature adults are at the lower levels. This theory is presented schematically in Figure 1.

Argyris (1957, 1960) and McGregor (1960), building on Maslow's work, asked the following kinds of questions: Supposing that many people at work have had their lower-level needs gratified, are mature adults, and, therefore, have higher-order needs that require gratification in the workplace, what are some consequences for employees and organizations if this is true? That is, if management's philosophy about workers is that they are motivated by lower-level needs, have an aversion to work, are unwilling to accept responsibility for their behavior at work, and must therefore be treated accordingly (controlled, coerced, and directed through tangible rewards and threats), what are the consequences? The answer Argyris and McGregor provide is that when the demands of organizations are in conflict with the needs of mature individuals, frustration, failure, and conflict often result. Employees react to these organizational disturbances by adapting their behavior accordingly. For example, behaviors such as turnover, apathy, daydreaming, and creating informal groups emerge. These adaptive behaviors, however, feed back into the formal organization to create increasing control and direction through closer supervision and greater specialization at work.

It was clear in Argyris's and McGregor's writings that not all people are assumed to be creative, intelligent, and capable individuals. Unfortunately, their (and others') writings have often been misrepresented and sometimes interpreted as suggesting that everyone strives and is ready for self-actualization.

Figure 1. Maslow's Theory

The Need Hierarchy	The Deprivation/Domination Hypothesis	The Gratification/Activation Hypothesis
Self-actualization needs	The stronger the deprivation of a need, the more it dominates in terms of importance.	The more a need is gratified, the less important it is, and the more important the next highest need is.
Esteem needs		
Belongingness (love) needs		
Safety needs		
Physiological needs		

Source: Maslow, 1954.

We would hypothesize, however, that faculty as a group would tend to fit Maslow's higher-order need structures and to be more mature in the sense of the word as used by Argyris and McGregor. We make this inference based on the nature of the teaching and research environment the academic desires and chooses to enter.

Alderfer (1972) presented a three-part classification of needs (Existence, Relatedness, and Growth, or ERG) that made explicit these individual differences in desires. His theory capitalized on the research generated by Maslow's theory, which had fairly consistently failed to support Maslow's propositions about the nature, number, and expression of human needs, at least in working adults. Alderfer's framework is presented in Figure 2.

An interesting characteristic of Alderfer's theory as shown in Figure 2 is that it explicitly considers, following on Argyris's works, the issue of frustration as well as the idea of satisfaction. The theory, then, postulates outcomes to be expected from behavior and environments which *increase* levels of gratification but also the consequences of behaviors/environments which *decrease* levels of gratification. Environments that facilitate an individual's need gratification will be satisfying, whereas environments that hinder gratification will be frustrating. But what is it about human needs that makes them so important and how is an institution to know which needs are prepotent for any particular individual, so that the "right" environment can be created?

There have been literally hundreds of studies connected with gratification of the Maslow-type need for self-actualization (Locke, 1976). Paradoxi-

Figure 2. Alderfer's Theory

Hypothesized Needs	Basic Propositions
Existence — all the material and physiological desires.	1. The less existence needs are satisfied, the more they will be desired.
	2. The less relatedness needs are satisfied, the more existence needs will be desired.
Relatedness — desire for mutual (sharing) relationships with significant others.	3. The more existence needs are satisfied, the more relatedness needs will be desired.
Growth — desire to have creative or productive effects on self and the environment.	4. The less relatedness needs are satisfied, the more they will be desired.
	5. The less growth needs are satisfied, the more relatedness needs will be desired.
	6. The more relatedness needs are satisfied, the more growth needs will be desired.
	7. The more growth needs are satisfied, the more they will be desired.

Source: Alderfer, 1972.

cally, the studies have overwhelmingly failed to support Maslow's five-needs classification scheme or his hierarchy of prepotency. This is not totally surprising, given that the perspective was designed to be a developmental theory and not a theory of only adult behavior.

The need theories of the Maslow heritage, however, do seem to provide a useful framework for understanding the kinds of people likely to be found in at least one type of academic setting, that is, a research-oriented one. These kinds of settings require people who are able to work independently, will set their own goals, do not require supervision, and have sufficient self-esteem to permit them to make their ideas public to a potentially ego-threatening world—the world of peer review. It would seem that these are the kinds of people who have developed, in the Maslovian sense, to the level where self-actualization is the need requiring gratification. The kinds of specific behaviors this need activates are difficult to identify but, following the career-entry issues discussed earlier, the kinds of environments required for gratification are fairly clear, and the academic world fits the description.

McClelland's Efforts

Almost totally independent of the Maslow tradition, McClelland and his coworkers (Atkinson, 1958; Atkinson and Raynor, 1974; McClelland and others, 1953) have pursued another need-based conceptualization of work behavior and economic achievement. The central need state hypothesized is the need for achievement (the others are need for affiliation and need for power).

Some interesting evidence supports the idea that people and societies which project achievement-oriented styles in their writings, artwork, elementary school texts, pottery design, and so forth, eventually are shown to achieve more in economic terms (for example, salary and managerial level at the individual level, generation of electricity at the societal level; see Brown, 1968, for an excellent review). In addition, there is some laboratory and field research which suggests that achievement-oriented work settings can be created that facilitate the display of any achievement motivation which people do have, especially settings that present a challenge, a moderate level of risk, and tangible indices of success (Litwin and Stringer, 1968). Finally, it has also been shown that some environments can inhibit the display of achievement-oriented behavior in work settings (where individual initiative tends not to be rewarded; Andrews, 1967) and that women may display their nAch through behaviors different from those engaged in by men (that is, through affiliative means; Stein and Bailey, 1973).

The findings of McClelland (1965) and his colleagues (1953) appear to apply well to faculty who join settings emphasizing teaching and research. These settings would appear to fit the description of an environment for high-achievement–oriented people, that is, one offering challenge with moderate risk. The challenge and risk of research are balanced by its frequent routineness, by the low career risk typified by teaching, and, for some, by the security of tenure. This is not to say that teaching is an unchallenging, no-risk occupation. On the contrary, teaching certainly offers great challenges for those who pursue it, and *for some individuals,* it may also pose high personal risks. The risks for faculty in teaching settings are self-imposed; the risks for faculty in a setting emphasizing either research or both teaching and research are externally imposed. Thus, peer review for the researcher is an ever present standard, and the probabilities of success are, on the one hand, lower and, on the other hand, knowable primarily only in the long run.

Need-Based Theories and Academic Motivation

For most of the need theories, unsatisfied needs are thought to be the activators of behavior. This energizing capacity of needs is thought to come from the psychological tension or imbalance created by an unfulfilled need. The behavior activated by the need state is gratification-seeking behavior. Thus, individuals are viewed as displaying and thereby exploring various behaviors until those behaviors that reduce tension and restore balance are found. We "know" which needs are active for people only through inference and attribution; we infer the nature of the need which activated the behavior by observing the type of behavior which individuals display in the absence of external constraints, and/or in the presence of a range of potential gratifiers. We infer a need for food, for example, by observing food-seeking and -consuming behavior. By the same logic, we may infer that people who persist in particular behaviors in the academic setting do so because the setting provides some gratification for particular needs or sets of needs.

By its unstructured and autonomous nature, the typical academic environment appears to us to afford the opportunity for people to fulfill any one of a number of needs, but primarily those needs which are developmentally the most mature. Thus, while need theories are probably not useful for predicting people's academic subspecialty, we feel that the nature of the academic environment attracts people who tend to be oriented to continued identity development through self-initiated behavior.

Following the need theories, we see that people remain in academe not because they actively choose to, but rather because they must; they must because the academic world is one which is likely to provide the environment in which the pursuit of the gratification of faculty needs is most likely. Which specific needs can be satisfied will differ across individuals and settings. In settings where both research and teaching are emphasized (the setting emphasized in this chapter), reality suggests that individuals with strong self-actualization, growth, and nAch can gratify those needs; people with more socially or affiliation-oriented needs are likely to experience frustration there, for, if they pursue teaching to the exclusion of research, they will lose their membership. For people with strong achievement orientations, who find gratification in research, teaching may be the cost of remaining in the "right" environment, and/or it may provide the security which turns a seemingly large risk into a moderate one. Conversely, people with strong affiliation or social-relatedness needs may become frustrated in the traditional publish-or-perish world of a research university and more likely to choose a setting with greater, or even exclusive, emphasis on teaching.

Whereas the theories we have discussed so far propose an end state which people achieve when their central need or needs become gratified, Erikson (1959) has proposed that a need for a sense of continuation of the self emerges as the final stage of human development. Although people are ultimately limited in their life accomplishments by their mortality, they can, he noted, nonetheless continue to have an impact on their environments through their progeny. For any faculty or teacher, then, a legacy may remain through the students they have trained. Erikson's view permits us to propose that as academicians engage in need-gratifying behaviors (in other words, as needs are fulfilled), continued fulfillment may be directed at developing others because this activity helps to ensure the scholar's continued existence. We suggest, then, that mentoring in academicians is another career avenue they take, but that such mentoring behavior is likely only in those who have been relatively successful in gratifying their central needs through their academic work, whether that work be teaching, research, or both.

But what of the academic who does not or cannot reach need gratification? What predictions can be made about faculty who are unable to gratify their needs in the academic role? All of the need theorists we have reviewed address the plight of those for whom fulfillment has been stunted. Maslow (1968, 1970) and Argyris (1962) are explicit about the "psychological illness" which can result from having need gratification frustrated. They suggest that, in extreme cases, when the inner nature is "crushed" or when a person is separated from the self, the pathologies produced may include: boredom, general depression of bodily functions, and steady deterioration of intellectual life. Less extreme, but detrimental nonetheless, are various forms of psychological withdrawal, such as decreased involvement in work and the work world, and greater emphasis on the material and monetary aspects of work. Researchers who cannot publish unless they work with others may, for example, respond to their frustration at individual achievement with an exaggerated concern over assignments and authorship. Teachers frustrated by their inability to conduct their classes as they expected might begin to denigrate the abilities of their students instead.

Alderfer (1972) also suggests a withdrawal from the source of the need frustration but his model permits redirection of behavior to the satisfaction of other needs. Indeed, as shown in Figure 2, he postulates that frustration of growth needs increases the desires for relatedness satisfaction, and frustration of relatedness needs leads to the desire for existence gratification; a hierarchy

in reverse is his proposal. Alderfer might predict that nonpublished researchers would turn to the challenge and affiliation available through teaching,
leaving the high career risk of research to others. Teachers might give up their
occupations for ones that at least pay well.

Only the work of Argyris and McClelland suggests positive and for-
ward moving alternatives when faced with frustrated needs; that is, seek satisfaction of the same needs by changing the environment or creating a new one.
For research academicians, this may take the form of physical withdrawal to
another institution or of acting to change the present institutional environment (through faculty unionization, membership in proactive organization, or
administration, in order to change policies) or of improving one's skills in
order to create a better fit with the environment (improving writing skills for
grant proposals and journal articles, attending symposia and conferences).
Teaching faculty, similarly, might move to another institution or assume greater
participation in administration and policy making or extend their education in
order to improve their teaching skills.

Because need theories are not very specific in their behavior predictions, it is difficult to say precisely how people will react to need frustration.
However, we can propose that general withdrawal from the chosen academic
role suggests frustration in that role and that such frustration is likely to result
in redirected efforts, some of which may be nonproductive from an academic
standpoint (for example, withdrawal to industry).

More specifically, Alderfer's theory suggests that frustration of growth
needs (through lack of research and publication) would yield redirection of
energy into more interpersonally oriented behaviors such as administration or
teaching. Failure to satisfy interpersonal or growth needs might, however,
lead to a preoccupation with material needs alone and result in such activities
as consulting to the exclusion of research.

Conclusion

This brief introduction to need-based theories of work motivation with
particular reference to university faculty has suggested that they are probably
high on the need for self-actualization, growth, and nAch. As such, they will
be attracted to moderately risky settings which offer them the opportunity to
be autonomous, to be investigative, to be challenged, and to be successful.
Some hypotheses were derived regarding the kinds of people likely to enter
such settings and be successful, and some of the consequences of success and
frustration. Specifically, it was suggested that faculty who have their needs relatively satisfied are likely to take on a mentoring function, while those who are
frustrated are more likely to redirect their energies away from students and
research.

One thing is clear from the need theories: In order to deal effectively
with the particular profile of the needs that the typical academic may bring to

the academic setting, colleges and universities must develop and maintain environments that permit gratification by providing a specific combination of attributes: for the academic researcher/teacher, autonomy in establishing the goals and means of research, challenge in the form of outcomes that are tangible and represent success, and some procedures to reduce the risk inherent in the above (like teaching or tenure) such that the entire experience is moderately risky in nature; for the teacher, active affiliation opportunities structured into the teaching role plus information about students—their orientations, needs, and directions of growth—permitting faculty to identify their own achievements and find the need gratification which results in mentoring behavior.

References

Alderfer, C. P. *Human Needs in Organizational Settings.* New York: Free Press, 1972.

Andrews, J. D. W. "The Achievement Motive and Advancement in Two Types of Organizations." *Journal of Personality and Social Psychology,* 1967, *6,* 163–168.

Argyris, C. *Personality and Organization.* New York: Harper & Row, 1957.

Argyris, C. *Understanding Organizational Behaviors.* Homewood, Ill.: Dorsey, 1960.

Argyris, C. *Interpersonal Competence and Organizational Effectiveness.* Homewood, Ill.: Irwin, 1962.

Atkinson, J. W. (Ed.). *Motives in Fantasy, Action and Society.* Princeton: Van Nostrand, 1958.

Atkinson, J. W., and Raynor, J. O. (Eds.). *Motivation and Achievement.* New York: Halstead, 1974.

Bess, J. L. "Anticipatory Socialization of Graduate Students." *Research in Higher Education,* 1978, *8,* 289–317.

Brown, R. *Social Psychology.* New York: Free Press, 1968.

Erikson, E. H. "Identity and the Life Cycle." *Psychological Issues,* 1959, *1,* 31–32.

Litwin, G. H., and Stringer, R. A. *Motivation and Organizational Climate.* Boston: Harvard Business School, Division of Research, 1968.

McClelland, D. C. "Achievement Motivation Can Be Developed." *Harvard Business Review,* 1965, *43,* 6–24.

McClelland, D. C., Atkinson, J. W., Clark, R. A., and Lowell, E. L. *The Achievement Motive.* New York: Appleton-Century, 1953.

McGregor, D. M. *The Human Side of Enterprise.* New York: McGraw-Hill, 1960.

Maslow, A. H. "A Theory of Human Motivation." *Psychological Review,* 1943, *50,* 390–396.

Maslow, A. H. *Motivation and Personality.* New York: Harper and Row, 1954.

Maslow, A. H. *Toward a Psychology of Being.* 2nd ed. New York: Van Nostrand–Reinhold, 1968.

Maslow, A. H. *Motivation and Personality.* 2nd ed. New York: Harper & Row, 1970.

Schein, E. H. *Career Dynamics: Matching Individuals and Organizational Needs.* Reading, Mass.: Addison-Wesley, 1978.

Stein, A. H., and Bailey, M. M. "The Socialization of Achievement Orientation in Females." *Psychological Bulletin,* 1973, *80,* 345–366.

Benjamin Schneider is the John A. Hannah Professor of Organizational Behavior in Management and Psychology at Michigan State University.

Mary D. Zalesny recently received her doctorate from the University of Illinois and is assistant professor of industrial/organizational psychology at Michigan State University.

Linking extrinsic rewards to teaching performance
can yield some important benefits.

Behavior Modification in a Loosely Coupled System: Thoughts About Motivating Teaching Performance

Walter R. Nord

The general task of administration is the translation of policy and organizational objectives into procedures and operational goals which direct the efforts of others toward the successful achievement of these objectives. While some administrators face far less uncertainty than others, few can be sure that any particular outcomes that they intend will result from their actions. In many ways, the degree of this uncertainty is a function of the degree of *coupling* among the elements of an organization.

Generally speaking, in systems which are loosely coupled (Weick, 1976, 1979), changes along any one dimension or changes within one subsystem will have fewer and/or less intense ramifications upon other dimensions and subsystems than would comparable changes in a more tightly coupled system. Consequently, administrators of loosely coupled systems are apt to experience considerable uncertainty when attempting to influence the behavior of individuals and units elsewhere in the system.

In comparison with most business and governmental units, colleges and universities seem to be loosely coupled. Moreover, in many respects the task of teaching is less routine and less measurable than many tasks in other organizations. Since it is often assumed that the successful use of behavior modification (B-mod) requires both easily measurable performance criteria

J. Bess (Ed.). *New Directions for Teaching and Learning: Motivating Professors to Teach Effectively*, no. 10.
San Francisco: Jossey-Bass, June 1982.

and tight control over the behavior of individuals we might be seeking to influence, B-mod may often be rejected as a viable approach to motivating teaching performance. While the use of B-mod is aided by control over a situation, I will argue that the approach has a number of benefits for administrators of loosely coupled systems as well (even those engaged in nonroutine tasks, such as schools). These advantages accrue from two factors. First, since in such systems the total amount of control available to administrators is apt to be small, in loosely coupled systems any additional source is apt to have important incremental utility. Second, there is a congruence between the way of thinking that B-mod stimulates and the nature of the administrative task.

In tightly coupled systems, administrators have many levers available for use in directing the actions of their subordinates. These sources of control are embedded in technology, rules and procedures, input and output controls, and so forth. Although unanticipated consequences are still frequent, administrators of these systems can have more confidence than their counterparts in less tightly coupled systems that, once their wishes are appropriately communicated, their subordinates will be constrained to act on them. Consequently, the *marginal* value of any incremental control over which a B-mod or some other approach might yield is often small in a tightly coupled system. In contrast, administrators of loosely coupled systems (especially those in which nonroutine tasks are performed) cannot expect high levels of certainty and do not have as many institutionalized sources of control. The marginal value of any increased influence to them is apt to be large.

Administrators of loosely coupled systems need to think probabilistically; they must be content with introducing stimuli and processes which produce only moderate changes in the probabilities of behaviors. In fact, usually they must think in terms of sequential probabilities; they must develop behaviors which are not the goal in themselves, but which are necessary before other ultimate behaviors or outcomes are possible. (For example, the development of a "professional" climate is not an end in itself but a means to stimulating participants in the system to behave as professionals.)

The B-mod way of thinking has one additional advantage for considering the particular class of loosely coupled systems in which colleges and universities are located. In addition to being loosely coupled, these systems are often characterized by a rather extreme form of decentralized power which permits members of the "operating core" (Mintzberg, 1979) — the faculty — to exercise substantial influence over many aspects of both their own work and the organization as a whole. (In other organizations these aspects would be controlled more unilaterally by managers or administrators.) Obviously, administrators of universities are not powerless; as Mintzberg observed, administrators in such systems often exercise considerable power, but they do it informally and subtly and move incrementally. Moreover, since they operate under conditions where other members of the system exercise considerable influence, administrators often must exercise their influence indirectly — by influencing one individual or group who may exercise influence on some third party.

Seen this way, administration becomes the process of designing systems and introducing stimuli which change the probabilities of certain behaviors which are themselves goals or which increase the chances that certain more remote actions will occur. One key question for the educational administrator which B-mod can address is: How can environmental conditions be developed which will increase the frequency and intensity of "good" teaching? Furthermore, because a teacher's colleagues are apt to have substantial impact on one's motivation to teach, the administrator must ask: How can the faculty as a whole and the senior faculty in particular be stimulated to contribute to the development of such an environment?

Behavior Modification and Motivation

The focus of B-mod is on changing the probabilities of behaviors. Users of this approach usually adopt an external perspective, centering their attention on manipulating elements in the environment to produce changes in behavior. They generally avoid making inferences about what "inner" psychological processes might account for the behavior. Consequently, they do not take the term "motivation," as used in psychology and everyday language, as problematic. In order to be consistent with this orientation, I will limit my use of the term "motivation." Instead, I will refer to the frequency and/or intensity of the occurrence of particular behaviors. When the term is used, therefore, the reader should understand by the quotation marks used that the external focus of B-mod is being emphasized (although I am not so radical a behaviorist as to ignore the notion that internal thought processes can affect behavior).

Even though "motivation" and the frequency and intensity of behavior may often be used interchangeably, the external focus and the emphasis on behavior have a major advantage for administrators: They encourage the administrator to specify what particular actions he or she wants. Such specifications, even if no other changes are introduced into the system, can have important consequences both in clarifying the administrator's own thoughts about what he or she wants teachers to do and in operationalizing the desired behavior for the teachers in concrete terms. For example, telling teachers that they are expected "to experiment with and evaluate, according to a specified procedure, the success of techniques A, B, and C" gives much clearer information than do such phrases as "being innovative" or "being motivated to try new things." This is not to say that, at least at present, "good teaching" can be made into a programmable task. It is only to say that it is both possible and useful to make many aspects of teaching (or steps leading to better performance) much more concrete than abstract labels of "good," "dedicated," or "motivated" teachers have led us to do.

In addressing the question of how teaching behavior can be modified by an administrator, I will consider four general approaches from the B-mod literature: respondent conditioning, ecological design, modeling, and operant conditioning. These are well-established techniques and detailed treatments of them can be found throughout the B-mod literature. (See Nord and Peter, 1980, for a more detailed treatment of these approaches.)

Respondent Conditioning

Pavlov's classic conditioning experiments with dogs provide the basic paradigm for understanding the process of respondent conditioning. Respondents are a class of behaviors which are controlled by stimuli which precede them. These behaviors include reflexes, glandular responses, and the responses normally called emotions. Usually these behaviors are thought to be governed by the autonomic nervous system and therefore not under a person's conscious control. For present purposes, the behaviors called emotions are of most interest.

Although it is possible to conceive of an administrator arranging pairs of stimuli to condition certain feelings or emotions, such an application is unlikely to be feasible very often. However, what administrators can do is try to design climates which are relatively rich in stimuli that are apt (via prior conditioning) to elicit certain desired feelings and, conversely, create climates which are relatively free of stimuli which are apt to elicit undesired emotions. Three possible sets of applications will be treated here: the development of climates generally, interpersonal processes, and symbolism and ritual.

Climates. Organizational climates have a powerful influence on people's feelings. For example, the allocation of resources to create classroom and other facilities which connote a professional, academic, or some other specific type of atmosphere may deserve far more priority than is often the case. Similarly, it becomes part of the administrator's role to remove stimuli which interfere with the creation of the desired atmosphere. While this approach might at first consider the physical aspects of a classroom building, it is apt to spread more widely to such things as eliminating duties (committee assignments, administrative routine, and so on) which are in conflict with experiencing oneself as a professional.

Interpersonal Processes. The respondent view also might serve to center attention on aspects of interpersonal relations that influence the development of a professional climate. In all phases of communication—written, interactions with large groups, and one-on-one sessions—large numbers of stimuli that elicit emotions are present. In each phase, administrators who have a clear image of the type of climate they wish to create can use communication not only to accomplish the short-run goal of information transmission but as an opportunity to present stimuli which evoke the feelings they wish to develop (and at times to avoid stimuli which evoke incompatible emotions) can be contributing to the "motivation" to teach. For example, use of words such as "colleagues" and "excellence" are apt to evoke quite different feelings than words such as "teachers" and "acceptable" performance. These different feelings will not only be evoked from receivers, but are quite likely to influence the feelings of the speaker as well. Clearly, these words are only examples of the general notion of how stimuli may create climates by the feelings they elicit.

All aspects of interaction, including nonverbal communication and the processes employed to disseminate information to obtain feedback, can be influential. In this respect, the value of the respondent view is not so much that it contributes anything substantively new, but that it directs attention to the possibility of influencing climates (very inexpensively) via everyday behavior—both by the deliberate and consistent use of certain stimuli and consistent avoidance of others. As with other applications of B-mod, a major advantage of the approach is that it drives the administrator to examine the current state of the system and to specify in behavioral terms the outcomes he or she wishes to stimulate.

Rituals and Ceremonies. The respondent perspective can center attention on a third set of topics—the use of ceremonies, rituals, and symbols. Pfeffer (1981) has summarized how a variety of these mechanisms operate in organizations. Sayles (1979) described a related set of activities in a leadership context. For example, Sayles noted how "leaders generally 'work up' the group to prepare them to be responsive" (p. 34). Both Pfeffer and Sayles observed how leaders enhance their influence by appealing to past successes and shared values.

Clearly, colleges and universities have numerous ceremonies and rituals which elicit strong feelings. Unfortunately, many of them contribute little of direct relevance to the stimulation of teaching excellence. Many of the ceremonies seem to be directed mainly at external audiences and not at the creation of a climate for learning (for example, athletic events). Other rituals, such as graduation, employ more traditional academic trappings that may elicit feelings related to teaching performance. Unfortunately, many of these activities occur at the end of the academic year and their effects dissipate over the summer.

Finally, many of the settings which might be used to present relevant symbols (for example, orientation programs) are addressed to many other needs and audiences. Administrators often fail to take advantage of them as opportunities to elicit emotions which would energize teaching excellence by the faculty and a demand for teaching excellence by the students. For academic administrators concerned with improving teaching performance, the search for ways to schedule and utilize ritualistic activities and ceremonies as opportunities to "work up the group to prepare faculty to be responsive" seems very worthwhile.

Ecological Design

Ecological design refers to the deliberate structuring of environments to modify behavior. Clearly, some of the ideas suggested in the discussion of respondent conditioning fall under this definition. However, ecological design also includes such things as the arrangement of spatial, physical, and temporal relationships and even of personnel to facilitate some behaviors and/or constrain others.

To illustrate the thought processes stimulated by an ecological view, consider the goal of increasing the "motivation" to be innovative and imaginative in one's teaching. Often a teacher's desire to employ a new technology is constrained by ecological factors (for example, a classroom in which all the chairs are bolted to the floor in long rows facing a lectern). The arrangement of schedules and personnel can similarly increase the likelihood that new techniques will be attempted. Clearly, variations in the "motivation" to use new teaching technologies can be influenced by the modification of features of the system's personnel, its physical, spatial, and temporal arrangements—in short, by ecological design.

Modeling

Modeling (or vicarious learning) refers to a process which is designed to alter the behavior of the observer by having him or her watch the actions of another person (a model) (Bandura, 1969). Modeling can be particularly useful in increasing the frequency and effectiveness of new behaviors and in decreasing the frequency of undesired behaviors.

The potential value of modeling for changing behavior is considerable. Teachers often may not try a particular approach because they cannot visualize how it looks or do not have a ready repertoire of backup responses. In such situations, one picture is probably worth well over a thousand words. Consider the use of a particular learning technique. Watching or listening to a model, in person or on tape, can provide the learner with a host of useful behaviors as well as a picture of the whole exercise. Such learning is apt to increase the likelihood not only that the person will try the technique but also that he or she will use the technique competently and hence successfully. Similarly, the opportunity to observe ineffective behavior can help the learner to realize how some of his or her actions may lead to dysfunctional consequences.

There are a number of modeling methods which can increase the frequency of effective teaching behavior. Obvious examples include films and role-playing. Opportunities to observe other teachers who are particularly skilled in some special method or style are useful in themselves and contribute as well to creating a professional atmosphere and demonstrating a concern with teaching excellence. They can act as stimuli that encourage teachers to discuss methodology and learn from each other. Modeling is already a proven technique for modifying behavior in industry (Goldstein and Sorcher, 1974; Hamner and Hamner, 1976).

Operant Conditioning

Operant conditioning is the best known component of the B-mod approach. I have deliberately treated it last in the hope of emphasizing the potential value of the other components.

The operant approach is concerned with responses that are normally considered to be under the conscious control of the individual. The most important feature of these responses is that they are controlled by stimuli or consequences which occur *after* the response has been made. For present purposes, an exposition of the details of operant conditioning (see Skinner, 1953; Reese, 1966) will be omitted in favor of examining some potential applications of its central principle—the arrangement of consequences following behavior to influence the probabilities of the specific behavior being repeated. Such applications require, among other things, inquiry about and specification of the particular behaviors which are desired and not desired. As previously mentioned, this process itself can make important contributions to improving performance. In addition, attention must be given to what consequences (positive, negative, and neutral) are available and how they can be made contingent upon the behaviors in question.

Hamner and Hamner (1976) provided a useful summary of how such a program might be developed. First it is necessary to define performance in behavioral terms (that is, what specific actions constitute good and bad performances). Once performance has been defined behaviorally, then a "performance audit" is conducted to determine current levels of performance. This audit often makes people aware that their performance is not nearly so good as they expected it was and makes them more responsive to a program for improvement. Stages 2–4 include setting specific goals for each individual, encouraging each person to keep a record of his or her own performance, and positively reinforcing desired performance.

Implementing the program requires that one know what consequences will act as positive reinforcers. (I will deal only with positive reinforcement in this chapter. For a discussion of the use of punishment, see Skinner, 1953; Solomon, 1964; and Church, 1963.) Positive reinforcers can be either internally administered (in other words, the person feels competent or satisfied with having performed well) or externally administered (material or social rewards given by a supervisor or through some organizational routine). Although traditionally operant conditioners have determined a positive reinforcer empirically (by trial and error), practically speaking, one can ask people what they would like and even rely on intuitive judgment and past experience to get cues as to what might serve as positive reinforcers. Once these are known, "all" that need be done is to make them contingent upon the desired behaviors.

I have put quotation marks around the world *all* to call attention to the fact that making rewards contingent on teaching behavior is no simple matter.

Mintzberg (1979) noted that while, in theory, competent performance of professionals in professional bureaucracies is ensured by fellow professionals, in practice such control is seldom exercised. Universities are no exception — in many systems there are strong norms against colleagues or administrators observing a professor's teaching performance in order to evaluate it. Consequently, it is very difficult to make rewards contingent on performance in the classroom.

This norm is in sharp contrast with the behavior of most faculty members with respect to their research work. Most are eager to have as many colleagues critique their work as will take the time to read it. I point to this inconsistency not because the situations are identical but because the research analogy may be useful in thinking about ways to improve teaching performance. The analogy suggests that, at least under certain conditions, professors seek criticism. In what ways could such behavior be enhanced with respect to teaching? Perhaps the analogy itself can provide a useful point of departure to stimulate faculties to explore these differences and examine their own behaviors. The analogy may be useful in another way. Clearly, one can choose people whom one respects to provide preliminary critiques of one's research. Perhaps if this volunteerism in selection were incorporated into the design of peer reviews of teaching, they would be more readily accepted.

While in many colleges and universities such systems will encounter considerable resistance, from the operant perspective their merits are clear. The frequency and intensity of behavior directed to improving teaching performance are functions of its consequences; the absence of contingent consequences is apt to be associated with the absence of the desired behavior. From the administrator's perspective, introducing such contingencies is a sequential task which begins with efforts to educate the faculty on the importance of contingencies rather than proposing any particular system or even proposing any system at all.

Of course, arranging to have consequences contingent upon performance is only one of many problems. One major question is, what consequences? Obviously, compensation could be made contingent upon performance, although some evidence suggests that such extrinsic rewards might actually reduce performance of intrinsically rewarding tasks (see McKeachie's chapter in this volume). The research on this matter is by no means clearcut (Staw, 1976; Guzzo, 1979). It may also be the case that many aspects of teaching are not intrinsically rewarding. At any given time, many teachers may not be able to perform well enough to receive the intrinsic rewards which are dependent on competent teaching performance; hence, the intrinsic consequences these instructors receive from teaching are aversive. Consequently, some sequential strategy which employs extrinsic rewards to reinforce behaviors which make good performance (and hence the receipt of intrinsic rewards) possible may be useful. Finally, the operant approach would agree with the position taken by McKeachie that greater attention needs to be given to enhancing the contingent intrinsic satisfactions of teaching. It encourages administrators to focus on all sources of rewards.

Although future research will undoubtedly qualify this assertion, it seems reasonable to assume that linking extrinsic rewards to teaching performance and the development of behaviors contributing to such performance can yield some important benefits. However, it is clear that successful applications to teaching performance will depend upon the ability and willingness of administrators to measure performance and to make rewards contingent upon performance. These issues raise some important policy matters, partly because often the unwillingness of administrators to make these discriminations seems to be responsible for their failure to develop and employ performance measures. Often, these failures are rationalized by the assertion that an unprogrammed activity such as teaching cannot be measured.

As a policy matter, administrators should be encouraged (or positively reinforced) to develop and use relevant performance measures. (Obviously, a precondition for such measures is specification of the desired behaviors and outcomes. Such specification by itself might have a considerable impact.) Moreover, policy-making bodies ought to avoid constraining administrators through compensation systems which leave little or no discretion for discriminating among teachers on the basis of performance. Clearly, blanket salary increases reward tenure in the system rather than performance. From the operant perspective, such systems result in an inefficient use of the resources we use to "motivate" people. Teaching performance can be improved by making rewards contingent upon desired behavior. Obviously, reviews of and feedback about performance by administrators can provide opportunities to give such rewards.

A second general matter raised by the operant approach takes the issue of misuse even farther. Often our systems not only fail to reward people for desired behavior; they actually reward people for undesired behavior or for behavior in conflict with the desired behavior. Kerr's (1975) paper "On the Folly of Rewarding A, While Hoping for B" makes this point well. Kerr shows how throughout our society we reward behavior we do not desire. To take but one of numerous examples, he argues that in universities we want people to work hard at teaching. However, the significant rewards (salary, tenure, promotion) are primarily contingent upon research. As another example, to the degree that reinforcement contingencies induce teachers to spend their time on routine administrative or monitoring tasks, they are "motivating" teachers to spend their time and energies in ways which are inconsistent with performance in the classroom. In short, we often reward teachers for A while hoping they will do B. It comes as no surprise to the operant conditioner that often they do so little B.

I will emphasize one other concept from operant conditioning which, I believe, has particular relevance to administration in loosely coupled systems. This is the concept of *shaping*. In simple terms, shaping involves positively reinforcing approximations of approaches to desired behavior. For example, consider a teacher who has fallen well behind recent developments in disciplines related to his or her field. Such a problem often requires a number of steps (for example, summer study, attending seminars, taking formal coursework, and so on). This teacher needs to be rewarded for taking these intermediate steps. If the administrator waits for the problem to be completely solved before giving rewards, the rewards may seldom be earned. What needs to be done is to determine a sequence of steps which appear likely to lead to improved performance and to positively reinforce successful completion of these—even though they may be early on the path to the ultimately desired behavior.

Conclusion

In this chapter I have argued that four components of the B-mod approach can be surprisingly useful in organizations such as educational systems, which are both loosely coupled and engaged in nonroutine tasks. It is important to realize that this argument can be made at two different but at least partially overlapping levels. At one level the approach offers a technology; at another level it offers an orientation.

At the level of technology the approach suggests some rather clearcut actions that can be taken. For example, one could attempt to specify desired behavior and to set up a system to reward it directly by making extrinsic rewards contingent on desired behavior. Similarly, one could establish a program to use models to develop particular skills. These activities are all possible with current knowledge and have demonstrated utility. This is not to say the applications would be free of problems; it is only to say that they are feasible.

As an orientation, B-mod encourages the administrator to focus on the relationship between external factors and behavior. In many ways, it is the orientation itself which is fruitful. For example, the program outlined by Hamner and Hamner is only partially based on B-mod principles as they are usually conceived. In particular, the use of goals is something which does not fall conveniently into traditional B-mod perspectives. In fact, one could argue that the success of these programs in companies such as Emery Air Freight (see Dowling, 1973) was due to the cognitive processes involved in goal setting.

The actual reasons why B-mod works are of both theoretical and practical importance. However, action need not await such knowledge; one needs only the orientation. The approach used at Emery was derived from an external orientation which sought to modify behavior by manipulating stimuli in the environment. The approach led people to specify what behaviors were desired and what stimuli were available for use, and to monitor the consequences of arranging these stimuli systematically with respect to the behavior. The orientation led people to administrative actions which were clearly productive.

B-mod, both as a technology and as an orientation, has demonstrated its value for the management of organizations. The notion that the B-mod approach may be particularly valuable in loosely coupled, nonroutine organizations is speculative but consistent with Child's (1972) argument that there are a variety of ways to exercise control in an organization. He suggested that where tasks can be formalized, control can be decentralized; where tasks cannot be formalized, control is often centralized. My argument is based on the assumption that in educational systems teaching performance cannot be formalized or controlled via centralization. Consequently, an alternative perspective for control, which centers on influencing the probabilities of behavior by the somewhat *ad hod* arrangement of stimuli, may be especially useful.

References

Bandura, A. *Principles of Behavior Modification.* New York: Holt, Rinehart and Winston, 1969.

Child, J. "Organization Structure and Strategies of Control: A Replication of the Aston Study." *Administrative Science Quarterly,* 1972, *17,* 163–177.

Church, R. M. "The Varied Effects of Punishment on Behavior." *Psychological Review,* 1963, *70,* 369–402.

Dowling, W. F., Jr. "At Emery Air Freight: Positive Reinforcement Boosts Performance." *Organizational Dynamics,* 1973, *1,* 41–50.

Goldstein, A. P., and Sorcher, M. *Changing Supervising Behavior.* New York: Pergamon Press, 1974.

Guzzo, R. A. "Types of Rewards, Cognitions, and Work Motivation." *Academy of Management Review,* 1979, *4,* 75–86.

Hamner, W. C., and Hamner, E. P. "Behavior Modification and the Bottom Line." *Organizational Dynamics,* 1976, *4,* 3–21.

Kerr, S. "On the Folly of Rewarding A, While Hoping for B." *Academy of Management Journal,* 1975, *18,* 769–783.

Mintzberg, H. *The Structuring of Organizations.* New York: Prentice-Hall, 1979.

Nord, W. R., and Peter, J. P. "A Behavior Modification Perspective on Marketing." *Journal of Marketing,* 1980, *44,* 36–47.

Pfeffer, J. *Power in Organizations.* Marshfield, Mass.: Pitman, 1981.

Reese, E. P. *The Analysis of Human Operant Behavior.* Dubuque, Iowa: William C. Brown, 1966.

Sayles, L. R. *What Effective Teachers Really Do . . . And How They Do It.* New York: McGraw-Hill, 1979.

Skinner, B. F. *Science and Human Behavior.* New York: Macmillan, 1953.

Solomon, R. L. "Punishment." *American Psychologist,* 1964, *19,* 239–253.

Staw, B. M. *Intrinsic and Extrinsic Motivation.* Morristown, N.J.: General Learning Press, 1976.

Weick, K. E. "Educational Organizations as Loosely Coupled Systems." *Administrative Science Quarterly,* 1976, *21,* 1–19.

Weick, K. E. *The Social Psychology of Organizing.* (2nd ed.) Reading, Mass.: Addison-Wesley, 1979.

Walter R. Nord is professor of organizational psychology at the School of Business, Washington University–St. Louis. In addition to behavior modification, his research interests include critical theory and the experiences of organizational participants.

We assume most employees will choose to engage in work behaviors that are rewarding. In this regard, are faculty members any different?

Expectancy Theory Approaches to Faculty Motivation

Richard T. Mowday

In a delightful article entitled "On the Folly of Rewarding A, While Hoping for B," Steve Kerr (1975) discussed the problems that arise when organizations establish reward systems that discourage rather than encourage desired behaviors on the part of employees. Kerr had little difficulty identifying dysfunctional reward practices in a variety of organizational settings. It should not surprise anyone familiar with higher education to learn that faculty reward systems in the university were among the examples Kerr highlighted.

The problem that is most often thought to be caused by reward practices in the university concerns the balance between faculty teaching and research activities. This balance has been the subject of increasing debate, both on the campus and among those concerned with larger issues of accountability in higher education (see Mayhew, 1970). While a full discussion of the role of faculty in the university is beyond the scope of this chapter, the nature of the problem can be simply stated. Many groups (often including, not incidentally, trustees, students, and parents, who must finance education through tuition and taxes) believe that the primary job of the faculty should be to teach students. This is generally true at the majority of state-supported institutions and may even be the case at some major private research universities, particularly as tuition increases the cost of education. But, even though faculty consider teaching to be an important activity, rewards in many universities are more highly influenced by scholarship and research productivity.

J. Bess (Ed.). *New Directions for Teaching and Learning: Motivating Professors to Teach Effectively*, no. 10. San Francisco: Jossey-Bass, June 1982.

If it is assumed that faculty members, like almost everyone else, are more likely to engage in activities for which they are rewarded, the consequence of such a system should be obvious. Faculty members may be encouraged to neglect their teaching obligations to devote more time to visible and highly rewarded research activities. The limited office hours posted by faculty but seldom met or the distinguished faculty member who infrequently, if ever, teaches students below the advanced graduate level may be visible manifestations of the problem. There is little doubt that effectiveness in teaching is held in lower regard by many faculty than research productivity, despite evidence which suggests that only a few faculty ever make meaningful research contributions (Centra, 1979). Morrow (1974) may be correct when he suggests that the prestige of a faculty member on campus depends less upon what he or she is paid than on how little the individual teaches, although one suspects that the two are often highly correlated.

The influence of university reward systems on the balance between teaching and research activities among faculty members provides the background for a broader discussion of faculty motivation to teach. More will be said later in the chapter about how universities can use rewards to increase faculty motivation. In the following section, however, attention will be directed toward a theory of motivation that helps explain how faculty members make decisions about where to allocate their time and how universities can influence these decisions. The approach taken in this chapter will focus on cognitive theories of motivation. More specifically, expectancy theories of motivation will be described and the major components and assumptions of this theoretical approach will be discussed. Following this discussion, an attempt will be made to apply the theory to the university setting to determine its implications for motivating more effective teaching by faculty members.

Expectancy Theory Approaches to Motivation

Expectancy theory has been the dominant approach to research on motivation in industrial organizations for a number of years (Campbell and Pritchard, 1976). In contrast to earlier motivation theories which emphasized substantive factors that motivate individuals (need theories, for example), expectancy theory focuses on the cognitive processes through which individual effort is energized, directed, and sustained over time. Expectancy theory attempts to explain how individuals make decisions between different alternatives or activities (such as spending time preparing a lecture or on research) and decisions about how much effort to invest in any particular activity.

While a number of theoretical variations on the basic expectancy theory approach to motivation exist (Graen, 1969; Lawler, 1973; Porter and Lawler, 1968; Vroom, 1964), the different theories make similar assumptions about people and generally share common theoretical components. First, individuals are assumed to have expectations or beliefs about the outcomes of their behavior. Second, individuals have preferences among the different outcomes of behavior. These two simple assumptions provide the foundation for more complex models of the motivational process.

To facilitate the discussion of expectancy theory, it is useful to consider a simple model of behavior-outcome linkages. Such a model, adapted from Staw (1977), is presented in Figure 1. The major linkages in the model are between task behavior or effort, task accomplishment, and outcomes. These linkages will be discussed in terms of the two major components of expectancy theory: outcomes and expectations.

Outcomes

Outcomes in expectancy theory are generally discussed in terms of their *valence* to the individual. Valence refers to the anticipated satisfaction that comes from receiving an outcome and this leads to classifying outcomes in evaluative terms (positive, neutral, or negative). Outcomes can also be classi- fied according to type, most commonly as either extrinsic, those mediated by sources external to the individual, or intrinsic, those mediated by the individ- ual. Praise from a colleague or a pay raise granted by the dean are examples of extrinsic outcomes; the sense of accomplishment that comes from finishing a book or the feeling of achievement that follows from a well-prepared lecture are examples of intrinsic outcomes. Intrinsic outcomes may follow from sim- ply engaging in a task (for example, the pleasure that comes from writing) or from tasks accomplished (the feeling of achievement).

In addition to the distinction made between extrinsic and intrinsic out- comes, a distinction is sometimes made between first- and second-level out- comes (Campbell and others, 1979). First-level outcomes are those things that follow directly from the job, such as incentives and rewards. Second-level out- comes are generally one step removed from the job situation and are thought to depend upon the attainment of first-level outcomes. For example, a pay raise (first-level outcome) may be instrumental to buying a new house (sec- ond-level outcome).

Considerable differences are likely to exist among faculty in the valence placed upon specific outcomes. Some faculty members may get little intrinsic satisfaction from teaching or research but may value the extrinsic monetary rewards that follow from good performance. Other faculty may place less importance on extrinsic rewards and gain primary satisfaction from the intrin- sic rewards associated with the professorial role. Individual values, goals, and needs are likely to be important influences on the valence of outcomes. In addition, the values held by departmental colleagues and the institution may also influence the valence attached to outcomes by individuals.

Making valued outcomes available to faculty is one major way univer- sities can influence faculty motivation. The success of such efforts, however, is likely to depend upon the availability of outcomes faculty value, the magni-

Figure 1. Behavior–Outcome Linkage

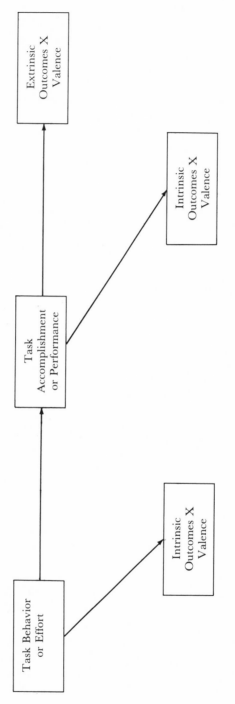

Source: Adapted from Staw, 1977.

tude of the reward, and the contingent relationship established between valued outcomes and behaviors desired by the university.

Expectancies

Expectancies can be viewed as subjective probabilistic beliefs about the outcomes that are likely to follow from behavior. Theorists most often distinguish between two types of expectancies. First, individuals have the expectation that effort put forth on a task will lead to task accomplishment. A faculty member considering writing a paper for submission to a meeting, for example, may have expectations that effort put forth in writing will lead to completion of the paper by the submission deadline. When the submission deadline is far off the probability of completion may be quite high. In the more usual case, where papers are put off until the last possible moment, the probability of completion may be low. The importance of this expectation in motivational terms is that individuals are unlikely to undertake tasks for which there is little chance of success. Where tasks are too difficult, or the individual lacks the relevant skills and abilities, or the time available for task completion is too short, individuals may simply decide not to engage in the task.

The second major type of expectancy concerns the linkage between task accomplishment and extrinsic outcomes. The most obvious example of this linkage is the belief that high performance will lead to rewards made available by the organization. For example, a faculty member may believe that the likelihood of promotion is high if he or she successfully publishes a book.

Expectations also link intrinsic outcomes with both task behavior and task accomplishment. Individuals generally believe that, for the most part, intrinsic satisfaction will result from engaging in an activity or its accomplishment. Intrinsic outcomes may be associated with both task behavior and accomplishment, or with one of the two (for example, faculty may experience little intrinsic satisfaction from grading exams, but may feel a sense of accomplishment, if not relief, when the job is completed). Beliefs about intrinsic outcomes are probably derived from the past experience of faculty members. When an intrinsic outcome is associated with task behavior or task accomplishment, the faculty member will have assigned an extremely high probability to the linkage, since it is he or she as an individual, and not others, who mediates the linkage (Staw, 1977).

Job-related expectations held by faculty can be based on information from a number of different sources. Past experiences of the individual, statements of tenure and promotion policy, promises made by deans and department chairpersons, and information provided by colleagues may all be important in forming the expectations held by faculty. It is important to recognize that the expectations held by faculty represent one major component of the motivation process that can be directly influenced by the university.

Overall Motivation

Motivation in expectancy theory is generally predicted by formulas in which expectations are multiplied and weighted by valence (see Staw, 1977). High levels of motivation are predicted by the theory when individuals hold strong expectations that effort put forth on a task will lead to task accomplishment and task accomplishment will lead to the attainment of valued outcomes. If either or both of these linkages are weak, motivation should be lower than when both are strong.

Expectancy theory has generally been used to make predictions in two different situations. First, the model can be applied to understanding how individuals choose between two alternatives. A person deciding whether to devote the afternoon to preparing a lecture or working on an article, for example, would be predicted to select the activity that is most likely to lead to the attainment of valued outcomes. Second, expectancy theory can be used to predict the level of effort individuals will put forth on a particular task. In this case the relevant comparison is between the expected value of putting forth a great deal of effort and the expected value of little effort (Staw, 1977; Vroom, 1964). If the expected value of spending several hours preparing a lecture does not exceed the expected value of taking a few minutes to pull together old notes, few faculty are likely to spend the extra time in preparation.

A number of studies have also examined the extent to which expectancy theory formulations can predict actual performance on the job (Campbell and Pritchard, 1976; Mitchell, 1974). When predicting job performance in organizations, however, it may be necessary to take several additional factors into consideration. Individuals with high levels of motivation are unlikely to perform well unless they also have a clear idea of the task and possess the skills and abilities to accomplish the job. Expectancy theory is primarily designed to predict levels of effort or motivation. When our concern is with predicting actual performance on the job (for example, teaching effectiveness or research productivity), the prediction problem becomes more complex and motivation is only one of several factors that may have to be considered.

Evaluating Expectancy Theory

Expectancy theory suggests that people are incessant information processors and that a conscious decision-making process precedes all human action (Staw, 1977). Consideration of this assumption suggests that expectancy theory may not be descriptive of human behavior in many situations. For example, think about how people decide whether or not to go to work in the morning. It seems highly unlikely that most people go through a cognitive process similar to that described by expectancy theory. Rather, most people probably go to work out of habit. There is probably a large class of behaviors — teaching in a routine way may fall into this category — that are more or less habitual and thus not the result of conscious thought processes on a day-to-day basis. Staw (1977) has suggested that expectancy theory may be most descriptive of behaviors in situations where (1) individuals encounter a choice for the first time (novel situations), (2) a behavior-outcome linkage that is habitual becomes highly unsatisfying, or (3) a better alternative becomes available to the individual. In other words, expectancy theory may be descriptive of certain important choice situations. Once a behavior-outcome linkage becomes well established, however, it may become habitual rather than the outcome of repeated conscious choice processes.

Applications of Expectancy Theory in the University

Expectancy theory has a number of important implications for how organizations can increase the motivation of their members. One useful list of implications has been presented by Nadler and Lawler (1977). Their ideas will be summarized and discussed within the context of what universities can do to increase faculty motivation to teach. In addition, the problems that may be encountered in applying the implications of the theory in a university setting will also be considered.

Identify the Outcomes Each Employee Values. A major implication of expectancy theory is that individual differences in desired rewards must be considered in attempts to increase faculty motivation to teach. Not all faculty can be expected to value the same outcomes. Some incentives such as merit pay raises and promotions may have more universal appeal than others. However, for some faculty members the chance to teach a particularly desirable class may be important and thus have motivational potential. The simple message that emerges from expectancy theory is that individual differences in valued rewards must be considered if motivational programs are to succeed.

Determine What Kinds of Behaviors Are Desired. While it may appear relatively straightforward to identify desired behaviors in the university, it is often problematic and may be at the heart of the problem thought to be caused by existing reward practices. The problem may take two forms. First, faculty may be told they are expected to do well in one area (teaching), while rewards are primarily given for performance of other activities (research). Second, conflicting signals may be sent to faculty about what behaviors are really important. Deans may tell faculty that good teaching is important, while the provost may indicate that scholarship is what really counts. In many cases, faculty may simply not have a clear idea of what they are really expected to do.

It should be clear that administrators who wish to motivate good teaching must articulate to faculty the importance of classroom performance. Unless it is possible to state unambiguously the importance of effective teaching, administrators should not be surprised or disappointed when faculty fail to engage in appropriate activities. Such a failure may say more about the university than about the particular faculty member involved.

Make Sure Desired Levels of Performance Are Attainable. Desired levels of performance should not be set beyond the reasonable reach of faculty. While this prescription follows directly from the theory, it may not always be easy to apply in the university setting. For one thing, it is often difficult to specify the desired level of performance. This may be particularly true in areas such as teaching, where it is not always clear what constitutes effectiveness or how to measure it. Moreover, performance outcomes associated with teaching (that is, student achievement) are often complex and may be influenced by factors beyond the individual faculty member's classroom performance. For example, the level of student achievement in a class may be influenced by university admission policies, the preparation of students in prerequisite classes, and the format of the class itself (for instance, mass lecture versus seminar). Thus, it is not only difficult to specify desired levels of teaching performance, but faculty contributions to the attainment of teaching goals may be problematic due to the multiplicity of factors that can influence student achievement.

Even when it is difficult to specify and measure performance, organizations can still take actions that help ensure that high levels of performance are attainable by providing resources which are at least conducive to (although they do not guarantee) more effective teaching.

Make Valued Rewards Contingent Upon Desired Behaviors. Perhaps the most important implication that follows from expectancy theory is that faculty motivation is dependent upon which behaviors get rewarded. As suggested at the outset of this chapter, faculty will tend to engage in those activities for which they are rewarded. If effective teaching is important, ways must be found to reward effective teachers and withhold rewards from those who are ineffective. This not only assumes we can define and measure teaching effectiveness, but also that administrators have discretion in how rewards are given. This may not always be the case. It is difficult to imagine how faculty members can be motivated to perform in areas the university considers important, however, unless administrators are both willing and able to make difficult decisions about who gets rewarded and who does not.

While the process of tying extrinsic rewards to teaching effectiveness is relatively straightforward, the ways in which administrators can make intrinsic rewards available may be less clear. Because intrinsic rewards are mediated by the individual faculty member, they are less easily influenced by the university. However, universities may provide faculty members with teaching opportunities in which the attainment of intrinsic rewards is more or less likely. For example, the opportunity periodically to teach different courses may provide greater chances for intrinsic satisfaction than teaching assignments that involve multiple sections of the same course year after year. Close relationships that develop between students and faculty may be an important source of intrinsic satisfaction. Most faculty gain satisfaction from the knowledge that students grow personally and develop intellectually as a result of their university experience. Moreover, most faculty are interested in the career progress and accomplishments of students after they leave the university. Where classes are large and student-faculty relationships limited to impersonal classroom contacts, the opportunities for intrinsic rewards in the teaching profession may be diminished.

Reaching a consensus within the university about important areas of faculty performance is important, but difficult to achieve. It may not be enough for administrators to stress the importance of effective teaching if faculty hold strong views suggesting that scholarship and research are the only things that count. Unless there is broad agreement about what constitutes important areas for faculty performance, however, the reward system may be circumvented and faculty subjected to conflicting pressures.

Rewards Must Be Large Enough to Motivate

Budgetary problems in many universities may make it increasingly difficult to ensure that sufficient rewards are available to motivate faculty. If the difference in rewards between high and low performance is not large, few faculty will see any payoff resulting from the extra effort required to become a good performer. However, the problem may not be limited to simple availability of resources. Rather, universities may have to make a commitment of resources to effective teachers. This has not always been done in the past. As Kerr (1975, p. 773) has noted, "rewards for good teaching are usually limited to outstanding teacher awards, which are given to only a small percentage of good teachers and which usually bestow little money and fleeting prestige." Fundamental changes may have to be made in university reward systems if faculty are to be motivated to become more effective teachers.

Universities may still face a difficult problem in motivating effective classroom teaching because the rewards that can be made available are not always as important to faculty as rewards that are controlled by forces outside the institution. Faculty members who develop national reputations based on their research, for example, gain recognition by groups outside the campus and may have numerous opportunities for travel and consulting. The ability of universities to offset the effects of these outside forces is limited, but it is important for universities to use the rewards that are available more effectively and creatively.

Expectancy Theory: Applications to Motivating Faculty

Expectancy theory provides a useful model to help understand individual motivation processes. Moreover, the theory identifies a number of specific steps that can be taken by organizations to increase motivation. Even though research on expectancy theory has been conducted for almost two decades, difficult conceptual and methodological problems surrounding the theory still need to be resolved (see Connelly, 1976). Despite these problems, one goal of this chapter has been to demonstrate that expectancy theory can usefully be applied to understand why some faculty members are not motivated to become effective teachers and what universities can do to remedy this situation.

While a number of prescriptive statements follow directly from the theory, it is suggested that applying expectancy theory in the university may not always be easy. It is also important to consider whether expectancy theory approaches to solving problems of faculty motivation are even desirable. The application of expectancy theory in industrial organizations has most often emphasized the importance of using extrinsic rewards to increase motivation. Some may take exception to the view that linking pay and promotions to effective performance is the best way to increase faculty motivation in the university. For example, McKeachie (in this volume) has argued that placing greater emphasis on extrinsic rewards in the university is most likely to result in lower faculty motivation. He suggests that intrinsic motivation plays a greater role in the performance of faculty members and that increasing the emphasis placed on extrinsic rewards may diminish intrinsic motivation.

In contrast, the version of expectancy theory presented in this chapter explicitly recognizes the importance of both intrinsic and extrinsic outcomes in the motivation process. The major conclusion that follows from the theory is that high levels of motivation are most likely to result when individuals believe that valued outcomes — both intrinsic and extrinsic — follow from task behavior and task accomplishment. Expectancy theory does make an assumption about the relationship between intrinsic and extrinsic rewards, however, that is important to consider. The theory assumes that intrinsic and extrinsic outcomes influence motivation in an additive manner. In other words, adding extrinsic outcomes to an intrinsically rewarding task (or vice versa) should serve to increase the overall level of motivation.

This assumption is controversial, since it conflicts with the growing research evidence that intrinsic motivation can be decreased by the introduction of contingent extrinsic rewards (see Deci and Ryan, 1980). There are several reasons why we may want to be cautious in generalizing from this research to the conclusion that extrinsic rewards should not be used in the university. First, most of this research has been carried out in laboratory experiments of short duration. Whether findings from the laboratory generalize to complex problems of faculty motivation in the university is a question that is difficult to answer with confidence. Second, some research suggests that extrinsic rewards may not always have a detrimental effect on intrinsic motivation. Although the conditions under which either a positive or negative effect is likely to occur remain poorly understood, the literature does provide some clues. For example, research indicates that extrinsic rewards may *not* lower intrinsic motivation when there is a norm for payment associated with the task, rewards are primarily informational rather than controlling in nature, are contingent upon "skilled" performance, and reflect competence at the task under conditions of high autonomy (Deci and Ryan, 1980; Enzle and Ross, 1978; Kruglanski,

1978; Staw, Calder, and Hess, 1974). As one illustration, intrinsic motivation of faculty may not be reduced when norms strongly support the linking of pay with demonstrably skilled performance.

Deci and Ryan (1980) stress that the mere contingency established between performance and rewards may be less important in determining whether extrinsic outcomes decrease intrinsic motivation than the message conveyed by the rewards. When rewards imply a high skill level or reflect competence at a task (in other words, convey positive information about the individual), they may be less likely to threaten intrinsic motivation than when the purpose of the rewards is primarily to control behavior. In fact, they suggest that extrinsic rewards that reflect task competence may enhance intrinsic motivation when the task is characterized by a high degree of autonomy and self-determination.

A final reason why we may want to be cautious about excluding extrinsic rewards as a tool for motivating faculty concerns our assumptions about the basic sources of faculty motivation. The nature of the professorial role, if not the level of salaries, suggests that *most* faculty members are intrinsically motivated. This may not be true for everyone in the university, however. Many people may enter the university for career-related reasons that have little to do with the basic love of learning and teaching others. In addition, some faculty who enter the university with idealistic goals may become disillusioned at some stage of their careers and thus lose whatever intrinsic motivation that may have existed. While some of these people may move into other occupations or university administration, the greatest number probably remain in the classroom. To argue that extrinsic rewards should not be emphasized in the university because they may threaten intrinsic motivation neglects the question of how we motivate faculty for whom the professorial role holds little intrinsic satisfaction. Motivating these faculty members may present the greatest challenge. It is difficult to see how these faculty can be motivated to perform at high levels without the use of extrinsic rewards, although in some extreme cases we may suspect that not even extrinsic rewards will do.

The university setting and the nature of the professorial role present unique problems in identifying appropriate motivational strategies. Unlike many members of industrial organizations, most faculty members find a high degree of intrinsic satisfaction in their work. Expectancy theory suggests the importance of establishing contingent relationships between faculty performance and rewards. Since intrinsic rewards are already high for most faculty members, this may suggest that our immediate concern should be the extrinsic reward system in the university. It has been argued that the effective use of extrinsic rewards may not threaten intrinsic motivation of faculty, although this is clearly a question that deserves greater research attention in the future.

References

Campbell, J., Dunnette, M., Lawler, E., and Weick, K. *Managerial Behavior, Performance, and Effectiveness.* New York: McGraw-Hill, 1970.

70

Campbell, J., and Pritchard, R. "Motivation Theory in Industrial and Organizational Psychology." In M. Dunnette (Ed.), *Handbook of Industrial and Organizational Psychology.* Chicago: Rand McNally, 1976.

Centra, J. *Determining Faculty Effectiveness.* San Francisco: Jossey-Bass, 1979.

Connelly, T. "Some Conceptual and Methodological Issues in Expectancy Models of Work Performance Motivation." *Academy of Management Review,* 1976, *1* (4), 37-47.

Deci, E., and Ryan, R. "The Empirical Exploration of Intrinsic Motivation Processes." In L. Berkowitz (Ed.), *Advances in Experimental Social Psychology.* Vol. 13. New York: Academic Press, 1980.

Enzle, M., and Ross, J. "Increasing and Decreasing Intrinsic Interest with Contingent Rewards: A Test of Cognitive Evaluation Theory." *Journal of Experimental Social Psychology,* 1978, *14,* 588-597.

Graen, G. "Instrumentality Theory of Work Motivation: Some Experimental Results and Suggested Modifications." *Journal of Applied Psychology Monograph,* 1969, *53* (2, Pt. 2).

Kerr, S. "On the Folly of Rewarding A, While Hoping for B." *Academy of Management Journal,* 1975, *18* (4), 769-783.

Kruglanski, A. "Endogenous Attribution and Intrinsic Motivation." In M. Lepper and D. Greene (Eds.), *The Hidden Cost of Reward.* Hillsdale, N.J.: Erlbaum, 1978.

Lawler, E. *Motivation in Work Organizations.* Monterey, Calif.: Brooks/Cole, 1973.

Mayhew, L. *Arrogance on Campus.* San Francisco: Jossey-Bass, 1970.

Mitchell, T. "Expectancy Models of Job Satisfaction, Occupational Preference, and Effort: A Theoretical, Methodological, and Empirical Appraisal." *Psychological Bulletin,* 1974, *81* (12), 1053-1077.

Morrow, G. "The Decline of Professional Morale." In S. Hook, P. Kurtz, and M. Todorovich (Eds.), *The Idea of a Modern University.* Buffalo: Prometheus, 1974.

Nadler, D., and Lawler, E. "Motivation: A Diagnostic Approach." In J. Hackman, E. Lawler, and L. Porter (Eds.), *Perspectives on Behavior in Organizations.* New York: McGraw-Hill, 1977.

Porter, L., and Lawler, E. *Managerial Attitudes and Performance.* Homewood, Ill.: Dorsey-Irwin, 1968.

Staw, B. "Motivation in Organizations: Toward Synthesis." In B. Staw (Ed.), *Psychological Foundations of Organizational Behavior.* Santa Monica, Calif.: Goodyear, 1977.

Staw, B., Calder, B., and Hess, R. "Intrinsic Motivation and Norms About Payment." Unpublished manuscript, Northwestern University, 1974.

Richard T. Mowday is associate professor of management at the University of Oregon. His current research focuses on employee attachment to organizations, including organizational commitment, turnover, and absenteeism.

Motivation to teach is higher in a program structure
than in a departmental structure, since program faculty
identify more with the ultimate "product" of the program:
fully educated and prepared students.

Organization Design and Faculty Motivation to Teach

Douglas T. Hall
Max H. Bazerman

While many organization design researchers work in universities, they rarely
consider the organization design of their own organizations. This chapter
deals with how aspects of a university's design affects faculty motivation to
teach. By examining how the "macro" area of organization design affects the
"micro" area of motivation, this chapter seeks to (1) expand the knowledge
base concerning the interaction between multiple levels of organizational analysis, (2) help university designers create systems that will increase faculty
motivation to teach, and (3) help faculty better understand their organization
and suggest innovative changes.

    Earlier in this volume Deci and Ryan proposed that teaching is natur-
ally an intrinsically rewarding activity. These authors suggested that a crucial
goal for universities should be to prevent organizational factors from nega-
tively affecting this intrinsic motivation. In agreement with this position, we
propose that the intrinsic motivation of faculty members is a cost-free input

    The helpful comments of our colleagues, Linda Argote (Carnegie-Mellon Uni-
versity), Philip Friedman (Boston University), John Hennessey (Dartmouth College),
Paul Lawrence (Harvard University), and David Schoorman (University of Maryland),
are gratefully acknowledged.

J. Bess (Ed.). *New Directions for Teaching and Learning: Motivating Professors to Teach Effectively,* no. 10.
San Francisco: Jossey-Bass, June 1982.

that universities cannot afford to waste. Consequently, we propose that as we begin to consider how to design an organization, primary attention needs to be given to avoiding the use of extrinsic motivators that will be perceived as controlling and to searching for external factors that will enhance faculty feelings of competence.

Organization (University) Design

Rather than trying to provide a review of the organization design literature in this section, we attempt to outline one framework that may be useful in identifying alternative ways in which universities can change organizational variables to increase faculty motivation. Galbraith (1977) sees organization design as the process by which organizations attempt to create a congruence among five strategic variables: (1) task, (2) structure, (3) information and decision processes, (4) reward systems, and (5) people, as shown in Figure 1. The notion of congruence implies that there may be no best way to design an organization, but that certain combinations of these five strategic variables (task, structure, and so on) fit together more effectively than others. For example, for a very unpredictable, uncertain task activity, a decentralized struc-

Figure 1. Galbraith's Concept of Organization Design

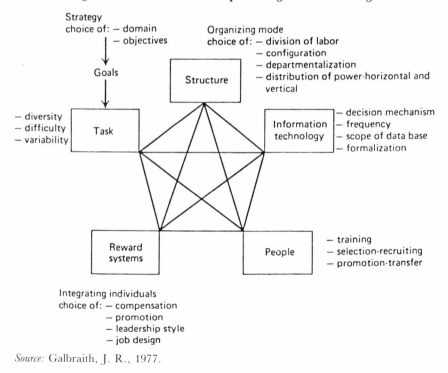

Source: Galbraith, J. R., 1977.

ture, giving decision-making discretion to the individual performing the task, may be more effective than a more centralized structure in which decisions are made at higher levels. Congruence implies that for a given set of goals certain patterns of task, structure, information technology, people, and rewards will fit more effectively than others. The choice of a given strategic variable is *contingent* upon the nature of the other strategic variables which are already in place.

Galbraith implicitly suggests that goal selection precedes design selection or change. We believe, however, that decisions concerning goals and designs should be made simultaneously. This perspective allows organizations an opportunity to examine the design cost and benefits of selecting a certain set of goals.

Goal determination is the most overlooked area of organization planning by the academic literature, strategic planners, and university administrators. Universities often claim to have a balanced emphasis on teaching, research, and community service. When we look at reward behavior (tenure decisions, for example), however, we often find "biased behavior." Our position is that university decision makers need to evaluate and communicate more honestly what it is that they want to achieve. We argue that university effectiveness can be best achieved by simultaneously identifying the goals of the university and designing (in terms of the five strategic variables diagrammed in Figure 1) the best organization to achieve these goals.

Organizational Design Strategies

A central concept in the study of organization design is uncertainty. Galbraith (1973, 1977) argues that the greater the uncertainty of a task, the greater is the amount of information which must be processed to perform that task effectively. Traditionally, Galbraith argues, organizations have reduced uncertainty and achieved coordination through three mechanisms: (1) rules and programs, (2) hierarchy, and (3) goals or targets. These are central elements of a traditional bureaucratic administrative structure (Weber, 1947). Using these three coordinating elements requires fairly "tight coupling" (interdependence)—a quality not commonly seen in most universities. Indeed, as March and Olsen (1976) have shown, universities are loosely coupled systems in which decisions result from a "garbage can" mixture of problems seeking solutions, solutions looking for problems, participants who come and go, and choice opportunities (defined as "occasions when an organization is expected to produce behavior that can be called a decision" by March and Olsen, 1976, p. 27). In this type of system, rules are minimized, hierarchy is at a minimum (only three or four levels typically exist between junior faculty members and the president), and goals are highly ambiguous and debatable.

What alternatives, then, are available for university coordination? Galbraith argues that there are two basic design approaches: (1) reduce the need for information processing and (2) increase the organization's capacity for processing information. The first strategy can be pursued by either creating slack resources (higher budgets, looser deadlines, buffer inventories, and so forth) or creating self-contained tasks (that is, organizing by output categories, such as academic programs, rather than by inputs, such as functional departments).

The second approach, increasing the capacity to process information, can be attained in two ways: developing vertical information systems (for example, targets, plans, budgets, periodic feedback reports), and creating lateral relationships (that is, informal links across different functional areas). Examples of lateral relations would be liaison roles (such as joint appointments), interdepartmental task forces, teams, integrating roles, managerial linking roles, and matrix structures. Galbraith's categorization of the alternative design strategies is shown in Figure 2.

How do these design strategies apply to a university and to faculty teaching motivation? Let us start with the premise that the ingenious feature of university design in the past has been its ability to organize the unorganizable: university faculty members. Professors are distinguishable in our society by their inordinately high levels of the need for autonomy. They also have high needs for achievement and security. The environmental climate conducive to satisfying these needs is what is called "academic freedom." Thus, given this type of person as the major line operator (deliverer of service) in the system, universities have generally opted for the design strategy of "information reduction." Higher education has seen conditions of relatively high degrees of slack (especially in the 1960s and 1970s) and institutions have been organized into relatively self-contained task units (schools or departments). Universities have not been known for their high information-processing capacities (vertical information systems or lateral relations).

Figure 2. Organization Design Strategies

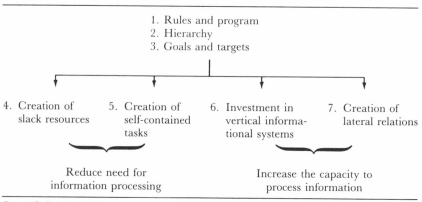

1. Rules and program
2. Hierarchy
3. Goals and targets

4. Creation of slack resources   5. Creation of self-contained tasks   6. Investment in vertical informational systems   7. Creation of lateral relations

Reduce need for information processing   Increase the capacity to process information

Source: Galbraith, 1977.

In recent years, there has been a major change in the design model for universities: a drastic reduction of slack resources (that is, extremely tight budgets). To maintain equilibrium, other parts of the system must adjust, or performance will decline. In the pages that follow, we will examine design alternatives for compensating for slack resources in the creation of teaching systems: more self-contained tasks, vertical information systems, and better lateral relations.

Case Examples: High and Low Motivation to Teach

To elaborate further on these organization design concepts as they affect motivation to teach, case examples might be helpful. We will examine one university organization known for high motivation to teach and one known for low motivation to teach — selecting from a universe with which we are familiar, schools of business.

One business school known to have highly motivated teachers is the Harvard Business School (HBS). HBS is nationally known for the quality of their teaching and the quality of their graduate business programs (Master of Business Administration, or MBA). Harvard is generally ranked first or second in the country in most surveys of MBA programs. The performance and career success of its graduates have been similarly successful. There may be disagreement on the definition of teaching quality, but there is little disagreement that HBS has it.

Goals. Why is teaching motivation so high at HBS? Let's start with goals. Given limited resources, Harvard places its strongest emphasis on quality of teaching. Teaching is primary. Harvard has a doctoral program, but, in our opinion, doctoral education is treated as a second-class activity. (In fact, it has been the object of external and internal concern.) Harvard does not have an undergraduate business program. It does have an extensive array of executive programs. Teaching quality is the number one goal.

Tasks. Related to this MBA teaching goal, faculty task activities are closely geared to teaching. Core courses are run by committees of the faculty who teach sections of those respective courses. Standardized course outlines, books, case materials, and exercises are often used. It is not unusual for a course committee to spend several hours each week reviewing and preparing for that week's classes. Team preparation may extend to developing a common set of questions to be used throughout the case discussion. Common evaluation activities (for example, a common final case) are often used. External activities, such as a limited amount of consulting, are valued for increasing the teaching ability of faculty members. Slack resources, such as support for case development, teaching assistants, time off for new course development, financial support for visiting lecturers, and so on are used generously to support excellence in the classroom.

76

Structure. Organization structure appears related to teaching activity as well. While there may be areas based on functional specialization (finance or marketing), the program or course committee (a self-contained task unit) constitutes an equally strong unit in the school. The power of a program or a course committee chairperson to structure the amount and nature of committee time, to vary the degree of course structure, and to evaluate other faculty and, in general, to shape the education offerings is considerable.

Information Systems. Information and decision processes are well developed in relation to teaching. Because teaching is such a central activity, the decision processes for revising the curriculum and individual courses is complex, time-consuming, and carefully controlled by the administration. For example, Harvard's new course in human resource management is the object of great schoolwide interest, not only because of its content, but also because of the fact that it is the first new course in the MBA core curriculum in twenty years. Information systems for improving and evaluating courses (for example, classroom observation by senior colleagues) are highly developed. The system's capacity to process information related to teaching is high.

Rewards. It is the reward system which most clearly reflects Harvard's stress on teaching quality. Promotion and tenure are highly dependent on teaching and course development excellence; research excellence is desirable, but not always seen as essential. This is counter to the reward system in most other high-quality business schools. Informal rewards (esteem from students and faculty colleagues) are also associated with teaching excellence: "Stars" are those who shine in the classroom, not necessarily in print.

People. People at HBS are both a cause and an effect of the strong teaching orientation. Faculty are selected largely on the basis of their teaching and course development motivation and skills, and these skills are further refined and rewarded over time. Students are attracted on the basis of teaching quality, and their expectations for teaching excellence are high; they also pay unusually high tuition, and therefore feel that they have every right to expect classroom quality. Because HBS is highly selective, its students are exceptionally bright and well motivated, which provides excellent "raw material" and intrinsic motivation for the teacher.

A Lower Motivation to Teach

Another excellent business school with comparatively lower motivation to teach is the Graduate School of Industrial Administration at Carnegie-Mellon University. Like Harvard, Carnegie is also an elite school and very highly rated, but it is not known for high faculty motivation to teach. Why is teaching motivation apparently lower at Carnegie? Carnegie places its strongest emphasis on research quality. It produces excellent graduates because it attracts excellent students who are self-motivated. The faculty's impact on the student's learning processes comes from the former's intellectual gifts (content) rather than their teaching skills (process). When academicians think of education at Carnegie, it is common to think of the production of research-oriented doctoral students, rather than businesslike MBAs.

The goals at Carnegie are noticeably oriented toward basic research and theory building. New faculty are advised that research comes first, teaching being a lower-priority activity. Faculty often work independently on their own courses. There is no formal course committee structure, only a loose area of structure. Furthermore, there are no formal departments that would "reduce interdisciplinary research." Power is based on one's stature in the research arena. Rewards (promotion and tenure) are primarily based on the publication of high-quality, high-impact research and theory. Poor teaching does not disqualify one, and through a form of reverse snobbery, low course evaluations may be seen as a sign that one is intellectually demanding and not about to compromise one's standards to satisfy students.

Information technology is geared to research activities (faculty research seminars, assistance with grant proposals, highly developed research-oriented computer systems, and strong contacts between Carnegie scholars and researchers at other institutions). Information technology geared toward teaching (classroom observation and feedback by senior colleagues, a course evaluation system strongly tied into the promotion and tenure systems) is not highly developed at Carnegie. Finally, people are selected and developed to fit with this style of organization: brilliant faculty who accommodate students while they write to satisfy colleagues, and students who adapt to a system in which teaching is not viewed as primary by their eminent faculty. (While there certainly are dedicated teachers at Carnegie who devote a great deal of time and support to students, these arguments apply to modal behaviors at the respective institutions.)

Current Issues in Design and Motivation

In the light of these examples and the organization design model, let us consider some of the complex issues involved in attempting to influence faculty motivation to teach.

Goals. The first issue, which becomes obvious in comparing Carnegie-Mellon with Harvard, is the problem of goal conflict. While most schools claim a balanced emphasis on research and teaching, teaching excellence requires trade-offs on other dimensions of university effectiveness. An organization that primarily attempts to maximize teaching quality will not be equally outstanding on research or community service because it will commit more of its critical resources to teaching. Emphasizing teaching leads a business school to run the risk of becoming a local (as opposed to cosmopolitan) institution, defining its own internal reality for members. This localism can, in turn, insulate a school from changes in the profession which it serves, which can hinder its long-term teaching effectiveness. Research performs an adaptive function for the organization, and an organization which downplays research does run the risk of obsolescence even in nonresearch activities. At issue is the clarity, balance, and salience of the twin goals, as well as the choice of the goals themselves.

Task. Regarding the task activities of teaching, with tightened resources we may see higher teaching loads, larger class sizes, more stress on basic, core courses and fewer electives (which provide more intrinsic rewards for faculty), and more demanding students. At the same time, we will have faculty who will feel increasingly underpaid. What we may have is a vicious cycle with increasing task (quantity) demands on faculty and decreasing rewards. This may result in less faculty effort and involvement per course and thus lower-quality teaching. In turn, this may produce more student protests and demand for quality, making the focus of faculty's work life even less intrinsically motivating. One result could be formal, negotiated agreements between administrators, faculty, and students on teaching activities which can be quantified: class size, number of office hours per week, limits on graded assignments, limits on outside consulting, and so on. Finally, optional faculty activities which contribute to the students' quality of life (participation in social events, counseling and advising, independent study courses, being available for informal discussion) may also decrease and, in turn, become the subject of negotiated, quantified requirements.

Impact of Student Culture. One factor which could mitigate these quality-threatening effects on scarce resources is the student culture. The norms, values, and informal rewards provided by the student culture can have a strong effect on faculty attitudes and, in fact, on the faculty culture. A student body that expects quality teaching and is prepared to contribute to classroom activities increases the intrinsic rewards associated with teaching. This increased participation, combined with the resulting increase in faculty intrinsic motivation, can substantially increase the quality of instruction.

We can begin by communicating to the student body the potential effects they can have on teaching effectiveness. Second, we can increase the likelihood of the development of a strong student culture by physically creating meeting places for students, and emotionally and financially supporting the development of student organizations. The more attention a dean devotes to student organizations, for example, the more power those organizations will have. Finally, we can bring the teaching and the culture issues to the attention of student organizations.

Release Time for Course Development. A critical task in teaching is innovation. Getting a sabbatical for funded research projects is common. Yet time to develop a new set of courses is rare. Why? Perhaps course development is considered by our educational system as a standard part of a faculty member's job. This task, however, when competing with day-to-day internal (teaching, meetings) and external (conferences, consulting) activities, often gets limited attention. We need to increase the saliency of innovations in teaching. Providing funded release time provides extrinsic rewards and information (signals) that can increase the intrinsic motivation from course development activities.

Structure

Organization structure can have a subtle but pervasive effect on faculty motivation to teach. Two of the most common structural forms in a university are a functional (departmental) form and the more self-contained program structure (analogous to a "product" structure in a business organization). Although the departmental form dominates in the university, the program form may be more favorable to teaching.

In the program form, faculty are grouped in terms of the program in which they teach (for example, specific degree programs, professional programs, executive programs). The program faculty would be a team, drawing on all the academic disciplines which are necessary to deliver that program. Our hypothesis is that motivation to teach is higher in a program structure than in a departmental structure, since program faculty identify more with the ultimate product of the program: fully educated and prepared students.

Most academicians have been socialized to believe in a traditional hierarchy. As Galbraith's model shows, various forms of lateral relations can increase the university's information-processing capacity. For example, the Harvard Business school and the Wharton School at the University of Pennsylvania have used a matrix organization, whereby each faculty member reports directly to program directors of the programs in which they teach and research, as well as to their functional (for example, accounting) department chairpersons. This creates an integration mechanism and vehicle for communication across both programs and functions. Obviously, these benefits do not come without costs — such as conflict, complexity, and so on (see Davis and Lawrence, 1977, for comprehensive discussion). Alternately, universities can consider less consuming methods of increasing interactions across functional academic departments. This might include interdepartmental course committees, interdepartmental task forces for special problems, the assignment of joint appointments or linking roles to key faculty members, or simply organizing teaching symposia of general interest to the faculty. As slack resources diminish and the need for information processing increases, new forms of lateral relations will have to be developed.

People

Composites of both students and faculties appear to be changing in the 1980s. Demographic changes are decreasing the number of recent high school graduates entering universities and increasing the number of older, more mature students. Another change is that more students will become self-supporting (through part-time or full-time jobs) as tuition and the cost of living increase. Thus, even though student motivation may be high, the amount of time and energy the student has available for school work may decrease. The changing student mix will require that faculty be more responsive to the needs of more assertive, mature students.

The second people-oriented issue which is emerging in many universities is the changing demographics of the faculty. With the postwar baby boom now coming into tenured positions in their thirties, we face the prospects of large numbers of faculty in a thirty-year, full-rank career plateau, with the concomitant risk of a frustrated tertiary faculty and a bored, if threatened, tenured group. A number of remedial and developmental activities are called for in the light of these changes.

Tenure Decisions. Many universities are currently facing the problem of an overtenured faculty. Coupled with the perceived necessity to reward (tenure) hardworking assistant professors, we potentially face a situation in which "new blood" and intrinsically motivated faculty may become a rare commodity in the future. We argue that a tenure decision can no longer be viewed simply as a reward, but must now meet the condition of improving the predicted effectiveness of the university in the long run. To do this, we will need more research on the best predictors of productivity of tenured faculty.

Matching Faculty and Tasks. The scenario of "deadwood" faculty being punished as the goals of the university change is a very common story. For example, when a university increases its emphasis on research, we often find the established teaching faculty no longer rewarded. Rather than view these individuals as the wrong people for the job, a more appropriate question to ask might be: What role can such individuals play under the revised goal profile? Typically, these individuals can perform many tasks that are needed in the new research-dominated organization (for example, course coordinators). We believe that matching the existing people to the appropriate tasks is an underutilized strategy in academia today.

Outplacement. Another common scenario concerns the ostracized faculty member who wishes to leave the university but, without the administration's support, lacks the contacts for successful outplacement. This is often a situation in which both the administration and the faculty member desire an outplacement but are unable to cooperate in the effort to bring it about. We believe that universities need to consider assistance programs that support rather than hinder such outplacement. Finally, Astin and others (1974) have even suggested the development of career (financial) insurance that enables faculty members financial backup if they wish to attempt a midcareer change. Such financial assistance would last for an amount of time that the transaction would reasonably take.

Rewards

What rewards are available to motivate midcareer faculty toward excellence in teaching? Money, promotion, chair professorships, and the like will be less available in the future. What can be done? As with others in this volume, we would argue that this reduction of extrinsic rewards may have the silver lining of forcing administrators to develop more of the potential intrinsic rewards in teaching. Three reward conditions (also discussed in other chapters) seem necessary to the development of intrinsic motivation.

Maintaining Faculty-Perceived Control. A crucial determinant of intrinsic motivation to teach is perceived control over the task of teaching (see Deci and Ryan, this volume). Consequently, we believe that maintaining faculty control and self-determination should be a guiding principle in designing effective teaching systems.

Maintaining the Joys of Teaching. Teaching is fun. Universities often create systems, however, that eliminate the salience of this fact. We believe that academic institutions should make sure that teaching remains enjoyable and that faculty members are not led to be so concerned with other factors — extrinsic motivators — that the fun — intrinsic motivation — of teaching is reduced or eliminated (see Csikszentmihalyi, this volume).

Establishing Clear Feedback. Clear feedback on performance is another vastly underrated, intrinsic, motivational method in most universities today. More feedback is coming now from students (on teaching), but much more feedback is needed from department chairs and deans on the quality of a person's research, teaching, and service to the school.

Still another option, beyond the three conditions listed above, is to have a clearly differentiated reward system with a differentiated faculty. It is possible to have certain faculty whose primary role is teaching and others whose main responsibility is conducting research. By giving visibility and recognition to teaching faculty, status distinctions can be minimized. With this structure, people who love to teach are not diverted by the notion that the only route to rewards is a long publication list, and excellent teachers are rewarded directly for teaching; it is not just an activity that comes "out of the faculty's hides."

Information Systems

Several issues of information flow have strong effects on faculty teaching motivation. Let us examine inputs and outputs of teaching activity. On the input side, the process by which teaching assignments are made is critical. If a professor is told what he or she will teach, without consultation or discussion, two demotivators could be present: (1) there may be a poor match between the courses taught and the teacher's skills and interests and (2) the nonparticipative process may reduce the instructor's commitment, perceived control, and intrinsic motivation in the courses taught. Some attempt to involve faculty in the course selection process, either by individual consultation or by group decision, is extremely useful in building faculty commitment to the course schedule. We argue strongly that faculty should be included in administrative decisions that directly affect them. This is particularly true as universities

82

attempt to increase their capacity for information processing through the increased use of budgets and other formal planning and control systems. For example, more management-by-objectives (MBO) performance-appraisal systems are now seen frequently in academic organizations. The more these systems are developed and implemented with high faculty involvement and participation, the more effective they can be a motivators.

On the output side (as Cammann argues elsewhere in this volume), feedback from information has a critical effect on the instructor's self-esteem and motivation. One type of feedback is the formal information from the course evaluation system. There is little question, however, that current course evaluation systems are extremely naive and unsophisticated in their design and underutilized in practice. The other type of feedback which is potent is the general reputation of the professor within the student culture. This may have more impact on the newer faculty, as more experienced instructors come to accept their reputations, perhaps with rationalizations if their ratings were low ("I'm very demanding in my courses"). Here, too, administrators have been slow in recognizing the motivational value of this type of information flow.

Summary

We have attempted to provide a theoretical integration of the areas of organization design and faculty motivation to teach. In addition, we have attempted to present a series of thought-provoking issues for consideration. We now add one final topic. If a university creates a change program to increase teaching effectiveness, it is advised to use an outside evaluator to evaluate objectively the changes that take place. Academicians are quick to realize the importance of independent evaluation for other organizations, but often forget that they, too, are biased human decision makers who may be incapable of objective evaluation of a program change to which they are committed.

We believe that we are entering a critical era for academia. Proactive change is a necessary philosophy for maximizing effectiveness in the coming decade. We hope that other researchers and teachers will follow our lead of examining the role of organization design on faculty motivation to teach. There is plenty of work to be done.

References

Astin, A. W., Comstock, C., Epperson, D. C., Greeley, A. M., Katz, S., and Kauffman, J. F. *Faculty Development in a Time of Retrenchment.* New Rochelle, N.Y.: Change Magazine, 1974.
Davis, S. M., and Lawrence, P. R. *Matrix.* Reading, Mass.: Addison-Wesley, 1977.
Galbraith, J. R. *Designing Complex Organizations.* Reading, Mass.: Addison-Wesley, 1973.
Galbraith, J. R. *Organization Design.* Reading, Mass.: Addison-Wesley, 1977.
March, J. G., and Olsen, J. T. *Ambiguity and Choice in Organizations.* Bergen: Universitets-Forlaget, 1976.

Weber, M. *The Theory of Social and Economic Organization.* Translated and edited by A. M. Henderson and T. Parsons. New York: Oxford University Press, 1947.

D. T. Hall is professor of organizational behavior in School of Management at Boston University. His current research deals with methods of providing career development for plateaued midcareer employees.

Max H. Bazerman is assistant professor of organizational behavior in the School of Management at Boston University. His current research deals with individual, competitive, and organizational decision making.

No feedback system can help teachers learn to teach more effectively
if the faculty and administrators do not have an idea of
what constitutes good teaching.

Feedback Systems for Teachers

Cortlandt Cammann

An evaluation committee is reviewing an assistant professor for promotion and can't agree on the quality of the person's teaching activity. With expressions of frustration about their inability to evaluate teaching activities they move on to considering the scientific contributions the faculty member has made by examining publications.

A graduate student walks out of a discussion section and says to another T.A., "I can't seem to get a good discussion going in that class, and I don't know why."

An assistant professor of philosophy is speaking to one of his colleagues and he says, "Oh, I save that lecture for the last class because my students really like it and it helps my ratings at the end of the year."

Two students are talking about courses and one of them says, "Oh, that course is a gut. The professor hasn't changed it in twenty years and it's an easy A. You won't learn much if you take it, but you won't have to work hard either."

These vignettes illustrate some of the problems that exist in evaluating and improving teaching abilities in universities and colleges. These problems range from an inability to give teaching activities adequate priority in decision making to a deficiency in helping instructors learn more effective teaching methods.

J. Bess (Ed.). *New Directions for Teaching and Learning: Motivating Professors to Teach Effectively*, no. 10.
San Francisco: Jossey-Bass, June 1982.

These problems have multiple causes. One of them is the lack of adequate feedback systems for assessing teaching performance. It is rare to find a teaching program with a system for measuring teaching effectiveness that is widely used and trusted by faculty members; there are few good models available for how these systems can be constructed.

In the past ten years, this area has received considerable attention, particularly from researchers interested in the evaluation of teaching effectiveness. Considerable progress has been made in the development of measurement methods for assessing teaching (Centra, 1975; McKeachie, 1979; Freedman and Stumpf, 1978), in the design of programs for using the information, particularly as a basis for instructor learning (Centra, 1973, 1977; Cohen, 1980; Kulik and McKeachie, 1975; Pambookian, 1976), and in the design of methods for developing complex information systems relevant for teaching activities (Bess, 1979; Stumpf, 1979b).

There are, however, a number of areas that have received less attention and that need to be considered when feedback systems are designed. What are the motivational consequences of having evaluation information used for promotional decisions? Is it reasonable to try to use the same information system to evaluate individual performance and to stimulate individual learning? Will one teacher evaluation system work in all departments? If not, what factors determine the types of systems that prove effective in different situations? These are questions that focus on the role of the feedback system in its organizational context.

While these issues have not been of central interest in the research on feedback systems for assessing teaching performance, they have been examined in more depth in other contexts. The purpose of this chapter is to consider the way this research in other contexts might apply to the teaching situation.

Components of Feedback Systems

The term *feedback system* refers to any standardized set of organizational practices and procedures that routinely collect and distribute information about organizational activities with the goal of facilitating effective organizational performance. Budgets, quality control systems, and formalized management-by-objectives (MBO) programs provide examples in industrial organizations; some systems for collecting student ratings of courses provide an example in colleges and universities (Freedman and Stumpf, 1978; Stumpf, 1979a). Such systems have three primary components that determine the way in which they function.

An Information Collection System. The core of any feedback system is a method for collecting information about organizational activities. Typically, this information collection mechanism is a measurement process that counts the frequency of events, assesses the results of activities, or records judgments about organizational processes. In the case of financial control systems such as budgets, the information collection system typically records the expenditure of funds by individuals or groups in a set of predetermined categories. In the case of systems assessing teacher effectiveness, the measurement often involves recording, via questionnaires, student ratings of teacher performance in a series of predetermined categories that reflect important dimensions of teaching behavior or course outcomes.

An Information Distribution System. A second critical element of any feedback system is the method for distributing information. This involves summarizing the information that is collected and providing the summaries to a network of organization members. Information distribution systems can vary widely both in terms of the nature of the summaries provided and in the form of the distribution network. The summaries can be quite complex and concrete (as would be the case for teacher evaluation systems that provide teachers with means and standard deviations on a variety of items and scales taken from a detailed, descriptive student rating form); or they can be simple and evaluative (as in a system that provides a department promotion review committee with a summary index of teaching effectiveness for a faculty member that was based on an average of all student ratings of teacher effectiveness over a three year period).

The patterns of information distribution can vary in terms of who receives the information and in the way it is made available. Some systems use a hierarchical pattern of distribution with fixed reporting mechanisms. Examples of such systems would include a budgetary accounting system that provides each manager with reports on the expenditures of their subordinates on a regular (monthly or quarterly) basis, or a teacher evaluation system that provides department heads with summary ratings of faculty teaching effectiveness for each course each semester.

Other systems are work-based and provide regular feedback to organization members about the outcome of their own work activities. An example of such a system would be a teacher evaluation system that fed back course ratings to teachers. Another approach involves developing data bases or reports that are broadly available to people who want to use them. Examples of this type of system would include a management information system where managers can get current financial information about their organization by asking for it from a CRT screen, and course rating books that students can buy which give descriptions and ratings of courses based on the reactions of other students who have taken the courses in the past.

A Set of Objectives or Standards. In addition to methods for collecting and distributing information, any feedback system must have a set of standards or objectives that gives meaning to the information collected. These standards or objectives provide the yardstick for interpreting the information and deciding what implications should be drawn from it. For example, a statement that a teacher received global course ratings of 3.5 has little meaning. It becomes more interpretable with the additional information that the ratings can range from 1–5, that most teachers get ratings above 4 and that all teachers are expected to have ratings above 3. Adding the information that in the past no person teaching the course ever got ratings above 2.5 and that the course was redesigned to create greater student satisfaction provides additional context.

The standards may be explicit or they may not be articulated; and they may be developed in advance or only after the fact. However, the standards must exist or the information from the feedback system will be useless.

Feedback Effects

Feedback systems can have a variety of direct effects on the behavior of people in an organization. The information they provide can help organization members better understand what is going on in parts of the organization that are outside of the range of their day-to-day experience. The information can provide a signal that tells people when something is going wrong and they will have to do something to fix it. Finally, when the feedback system provides organization members with information on their own performance, it can provide an incentive to perform better or a source of internal satisfaction for a job well done.

In addition to these possible direct effects of feedback system information, the way in which the feedback system is designed and used can have important effects on the people in organizations. If the system is used to integrate people into an organization by involving them in the process of setting goals, identifying problems, developing solutions and monitoring their effectiveness, then feedback systems can increase an organization member's commitment to the organization and intrinsic motivation to perform well (Hackman and Oldham, 1980; Lawler and Rhode, 1976). If the feedback information is used as a basis for providing organizational rewards and penalties, it can increase an organization member's desire to perform well on the feedback system measures. This can provide an inducement to perform well, or to manipulate the measurement system by keeping the goals and standards low, for example, or by concentrating effort in measured areas and ignoring unmeasured ones (Cammann, 1976; Hofstede, 1967; Jasinski, 1956; Lawler and Rhode, 1976; Likert, 1967).

Finally, if the feedback system is used to help organization members discover, in concrete terms, the effects of their behavior, and if it is used as a tool for providing support for experimentation and learning, a feedback system can help create conditions that will facilitate learning and the explanation of new modes of behavior (see Argyris and Schön, 1978, for a more detailed discussion of the conditions that will facilitate organizational learning). If, however, the system is used to punish failure, and to reinforce efficient performance of prespecified outcomes through the use of standardized methods, the feedback system will inhibit learning and promote standardization.

The actual effects of a specific feedback system on organization members will depend on a variety of factors. These include the nature of the feedback system design, the use of the system, and the general climate and context of the organization. It can be expected that the effects of any particular design or usage pattern will vary as the organizational conditions vary (Hopwood, 1973), and that designing an effective feedback system involves developing a system whose design, purpose and use are appropriate for the organization in which it is being used.

Designing Feedback Systems for Teaching Situations

A key problem facing people interested in designing feedback systems for teaching situations is to discover designs and usage patterns that will create motivational effects that are consistent with the system's intended purposes. Thus, in a university setting, a feedback system that motivates faculty to experiment with new teaching methods and to involve students in the learning process would be effective if the system is intended to produce standardized approaches to teaching specific content in a cost effective manner. Similarly, a feedback system designed to provide promotion review committees with valid information about teaching competence will be effective if it provides accurate information in a timely manner, but not if it motivates faculty to distort the information on which the system is based or if it motivates faculty who can teach well to leave and find other jobs.

There are a number of problems that must be addressed by people interested in designing effective feedback systems for teaching situations. Some of these involve the design of the system components; some involve the congruence among the purposes for having the system; and some involve the mission and strategy of the departments where the system will be used.

Reliability issues are of three types: scope of measurement, validity of measurement, and influenceability of measurement. The information collected should, to the extent possible, reflect all of the behavior that is relevant for the users of the information; the information collected should provide an accurate description of the behaviors or consequences being assessed; and the information should only be influenced by changes in behavior or performance, not by strategies designed to directly manipulate the information without improving performance. While an ideal measurement system would always have these characteristics, their importance will vary depending on the intended uses of the information. When the feedback is being used by people who are not intimately familiar with what is going on in the classroom (promotion committees or prospective students) scope and accuracy are more important because the feedback system will represent one of the major sources of information. If the users are more directly familiar with what is going on in courses (teachers, participating students, administrators that observe classroom activities) scope and accuracy are less critical because the users have their own direct experience to supplement the feedback information. Similarly, influencability of the measures will be more critical if the intended users of the system will motivate faculty to manipulate the information going into the system, but not if the faculty have an interest in seeing that the information is as accurate as possible.

In designing the information distribution system, the critical issues involve utility and standardization. To be useful, the distribution system must provide information to the people who need it in a timely manner and in a form that they can use. Determining what patterns of distribution pattern will serve these functions will obviously depend on the local situation; but if the information goes to the wrong people, does not arrive when it is needed, or isn't in a form that people can understand and use, the system will obviously be ineffective. It is obvious that these issues must be carefully considered when the system is first developed, but it is equally important that they be reviewed on a regular basis. As courses change, administrative practices change and as the characteristics of user populations evolve, the information needs will vary and if the distribution system is not regularly reviewed, its appropriateness and value can deteriorate.

In designing this goal/standard setting system, the critical issues involve congruence between the feedback system, its factors, and the broader organizational context. If the purpose of the feedback system is to allow comparisons among courses or teachers, it is important that the goals or standards be relatively uniform and valid. This probably means that criterion based on norm based standards should be used and that they should be centrally set in a way that takes into account effects of factors such as class size, course level, and topical content (Kulik and McKeachie, 1975). If the purpose is to encourage intrinsic commitment to good teaching performance or to facilitate teacher learning, the goal setting process should be more individually based, involving teachers in setting concrete goals for their courses that they will try to meet and providing for a regular review of the consequences that result. In addition, the goal setting process should be congruent with the norms of the faculty for making curriculum related decisions. This latter issue is a potential problem in many university settings since the norms around teaching often stress individual academic freedom and are often supported by goal setting systems that minimize discussion of course content among faculty and administrators.

In general, the problems involved in developing adequate feedback systems for monitoring teaching activities do not appear insurmountable. There are technical problems involved in developing information collection and distribution systems, but a good deal of work has been done to develop acceptable solutions. Developing systems that fit the context can also involve problems, but these can probably be handled if the system designers carefully analyze the systems' purpose and the requirements of the setting.

A more substantial problem appears to be getting the resources required to design and maintain an effective system. These tasks are likely to require the time and energy of faculty and administrators, the cooperation of students, and the use of university resources — all of these can be difficult to acquire. Yet without them the feedback systems are unlikely to be effective. Thus, while it seems likely that useful feedback systems can be designed, administrators and designers need to be aware of the costs involved to develop and maintain them and carefully evaluate the commitment required before such systems are implemented.

Congruence Issues. Because of the time, energy and resources required to develop and maintain an effective feedback system, there is a temptation to try to design systems that can serve multiple functions. While some researchers have identified the difficulties involved in doing this in teaching situations (Kulik and McKeachie, 1975; McKeachie, 1979) others have tried to develop designs that can be used a variety of different ways (Stumpf, 1979a, 1979b). The research on feedback systems in other contexts suggests that while such systems can probably perform multiple functions, the congruence of their functions may be important. In particular, it seems likely that there are two generic sets of functions which are internally compatible, but not easily mixed. The first set involves the functions of learning and adaptation, intrinsic motivation and participative control, and information distribution where the recipients of the information do not make decisions that threaten faculty interests. Each of these functions of feedback systems provides minimal threat to faculty members, can be served with relatively descriptive feedback information, and can be carried out in a way that is consistent with norms of participation and faculty involvement in decision making. Thus it seems likely that a simple system could be designed that would produce complementary motivational effects and organizational outcomes as long as the organizational context was supportive of participative, collaborative decision making.

The second set involves the functions of extrinsic motivation and external control, and the distribution of information to decision makers who have to evaluate faculty performance. Systems designed to perform each of these functions give faculty an extrinsic reason to perform well on feedback systems indicators and reinforce the structure of authority within the department or school. They require valid, evaluative measurement systems that can not be easily manipulated and will probably be most effective when objective or legitimate standards exist. Such systems can probably be used in participative or democratic contexts if the decisions governing their operation are generally agreed to by the faculty (Thorne, 1980), but they can also be effective in more autocratic contexts when they reinforce the existing structures of authority.

If a single feedback system is used to serve both sets of functions, dysfunctions may result. For example, using feedback information for evaluative purposes may reduce the faculty's experience of autonomy and therefore their intrinsic motivation to perform well. It may also increase the salience of performing well on performance indicators and reduce willingness to risk trying new teaching methods. Similarly, the use of participation in setting goals to increase intrinsic motivation or facilitate learning may reduce the validity of the goals used in making pay and promotion decisions. The result may be the setting of easy goals, which reduces their motivational effectiveness.

If these conclusions are correct, they suggest that the same feedback system should not be used for purposes of facilitating faculty learning and for faculty evaluation. If both objectives are important, separate feedback systems should be designed. It is not clear whether it is reasonable to expect both systems to work in the same departments; but it seems possible that they could as long as they are sufficiently independent of each other and they are both designed to be congruent with the overall climate that exists. Separate systems, however, increase the costs in faculty, student, and administrator's time and energy — costs which are usually unwillingly borne.

Mission and Strategy Issues. Feedback systems are an organizational tool that can help organizations function effectively. To perform this function, however, the mission and strategy must be clear, at least in the domains relevant for the feedback system. No feedback system can help teachers learn to teach more effectively if the faculty and administrators do not have an idea of what constitutes good teaching. No feedback system can be used effectively to control the performance of teachers if the people exercising control do not have an idea of the type of behavior and performance they desire. No feedback system can provide administrators, faculty, or students with information that will aid their decision making if these people do not know what decisions they are making or what information they need to use in making them. In order for a feedback system to be effective, people must be clear about the organizational purposes that it is designed to support and about the nature of their role in achieving them.

In many academic departments, faculty are not clear about the mission of the department, the strategy that is being used to accomplish it, and the structure that should exist to facilitate the execution of the strategy. In such situations it will be difficult to design a feedback system that will be effective. The first step in developing a feedback system may have to be an intervention into the department itself to get sufficient clarity about what the department is trying to accomplish and how it is organized so that the feedback system can be diverse, ranging from a clear understanding that the organization will be loosely organized and will allow maximum faculty autonomy within generally agreed to parameters, to an agreement that highly centralized decision making and control should characterize the department's process. Once these issues are clarified, an appropriate feedback system can be designed.

Research Directions

The application of feedback systems research from other contexts suggests a number of important research questions that need to be answered about the design of feedback systems for teaching. Are faculty motivated to accomplish feedback system goals rather than high performance when the systems are used for exercising external control or making evaluative decisions? It is possible that faculty are professionally trained and committed to the values of effective teaching, and that, as a result, such goal displacement will not occur. Research on the nature of faculty responses would be quite useful in finding out.

Which feedback system designs will be congruent with different departmental norms and practices? When faculty are largely independent, it seems likely that an appropriate design is to make feedback systems and expert help available, but not required, for improving teaching; when faculty work closely together to determine curriculum purpose and design, it seems that a more participative process of setting learning goals for each course and testing their accomplishment might be very effective. Are these hypotheses correct? Research examining the effects of different designs under different conditions and the nature of the process that is effective for developing designs that fit any particular department would be very helpful for answering such questions and providing guidance to administrators who are interested in getting such systems into place.

Can feedback systems and departments be designed so that a single feedback system can serve a range of purposes? It seems possible that there exist feedback system designs and departmental practices that would allow a single feedback system to serve multiple purposes, including the facilitation of both learning and evaluation. Such a system would require each individual to recognize that the department requires both types of activities and to accept responsibility for helping them to occur as validly and efficiently as possible. In such a circumstance it might well be possible to design a single feedback system that would be used for a wide range of purposes without creating conflicts that destroy the system's utility. Research examining the possibility of creating such systems and the nature of the structures and processes that could make them work could make a valuable contribution to our understanding of how effective departments can be designed and how feedback systems can be used to improve their effectiveness.

What factors lead departments to resist the development of effective feedback systems? Clearly one implication of the arguments presented in this chapter is that if a department does not now have effective feedback systems, it is not because of a lack of technology. Enough is known about feedback system design that effective systems can be developed. Why then haven't they been? What sources of resistance need to be overcome and what are the basic methods for doing so? These are questions that need answers if teaching departments are to succeed in developing effective feedback systems.

Much is currently known about how feedback systems can be designed and used. There is, however, much we need to know about how they should be integrated into departmental contexts and how departmental contexts should be organized before we can expect to develop and implement successful feedback systems.

94

References

Argyris, C., and Schön, D. A. *Organizational Learning: A Theory of Action in Perspective.* Reading, Mass.: Addison-Wesley, 1978.

Bess, J. L. "Classroom and Management Decisions Using Student Data." *Journal of Higher Education,* 1979, *50* (3), 256–279.

Cammann, C. "Effects of the Use of Control Systems." *Accounting, Organizations and Society,* 1976, *1* (4), 301–313.

Centra, J. A. "Effectiveness of Student Feedback in Modifying College Instruction." *Journal of Educational Psychology,* 1973, *65* (3), 395–401.

Centra, J. A. "Colleagues as Raters of Classroom Instruction." *Journal of Higher Education,* 1975, *46* (1), 327–337.

Centra, J. A. "The How and Why of Evaluating Teaching." *New Directions for Higher Education,* 1977, *17,* 93–106.

Cohen, P. A. "Effectiveness of Student-Rating Feedback for Improving College Instruction: A Meta-Analysis of Findings." *Research in Higher Education,* 1980, *13* (4), 321–341.

Freedman, R. D., and Stumpf, S. A. "Student Evaluations of Courses and Faculty Based on a Perceived Learning Criterion: Scale Construction, Validation, and Comparison of Results." *Applied Psychological Measurement,* 1978, *2* (2), 189–202.

Hackman, J. R., and Oldham, G. R. *Work Redesign.* Reading, Mass.: Addison-Wesley, 1980.

Hofstede, G. H. *The Game of Budget Control.* Assen, Netherlands: Van Gorcum, 1967.

Hopwood, A. G. *An Accounting System and Managerial Behavior.* Lexington, Mass.: Lexington Books, 1973.

Jasinski, F. J. "Use and Misuse of Efficiency Controls." *Harvard Business Review,* 1956, *34* (4), 105–112.

Kulik, J. A., and McKeachie, W. J. "The Evaluation of Teachers in Higher Education." In F. N. Kerlinger (Ed.), *Review of Research in Education* (Vol. 3). Itasca, Ill.: Peacock Publishers, 1975.

Lawler, E. E. III, and Rhode, J. G. *Information and Control in Organizations.* Pacific Palisades, Calif.: Goodyear, 1976.

Likert, R. *The Human Organization.* New York: McGraw-Hill, 1967.

McKeachie, W. J. "Student Ratings of Faculty: A Reprise." *Academe,* 1979, *65* (6), 384–397.

Pambookian, H. S. "Discrepancy Between Instructor and Student Evalutions of Instruction: Effect on Instructor." *Instructional Science,* 1976, *5* (1), 63–75.

Stumpf, S. A. "Assessing Academic Program and Department Effectiveness Using Student Evaluation Data." *Research in Higher Education,* 1979a, *11* (4), 353–363.

Stumpf, S. A. "Student Evaluations of NYU/GBA Courses and Faculty: A Review, Departmental Comparisons and Time-Sharing Access to CFI Data." Working paper, New York University Graduate School of Business Administration, 1979b, pp. 79–95.

Thorne, G. L. "Student Ratings of Instructors: From Scores to Administrative Decisions." *Journal of Higher Education,* 1980, *51* (2), 207–214.

Cortlandt Cammann is associate research scientist at the Institute for Social Research of the University of Michigan. His research has focused on the ways people behave in different organizational settings and on the effects of control systems on behavior.

Do faculty pass through career stages that affect their motivation to teach?

Career Phases and Their Influence on Faculty Motivation

Robert T. Blackburn

The popular as well as the scholarly press increasingly calls attention to changes in adult development. Some speak of passages, others of seasons, and still others of cycles that adults are said inevitably to pass through, periods of flux and times of stability, phases of stress and stages of relative serenity. To the extent that such time intervals do exist and change, one reasonably expects motivations vis a vis a person's work roles also to undergo change, including motivation to teach.

While it may seem pedantic to raise the question of whether or not career phases exist since most academics will quickly give an affirmative answer, the question is not a rhetorical one. Faculty indeed speak of productive and dry periods, of exciting and dull classes; it is also true that academic life is structured to allow renewal with its change of terms, courses offered, and students taught. Leaves, different assignments, even the year itself—the "academic" year—are all designed to accommodate and to precipitate phase changes.

If there were clearly identifiable career phases for college professors, effective administrators could find ways to alter an individual's institutional responsibilities during a phase when motivations were low so as to maintain high teaching performance throughout the organization. In addition, or alter-

J. Bess (Ed.). *New Directions for Teaching and Learning: Motivating Professors to Teach Effectively*, no. 10. San Francisco: Jossey-Bass, June 1982.

natively, counseling might be able to change, or else mitigate, low motivation periods. Particularly high motivation phases could be capitalized upon for the benefit of the individual and the college. Unfortunately, there is little demonstrable evidence to support the existence of phases.*

Direct Evidence

Assuming that there exists a high correlation between motivation and performance (see other chapters in this book) and that student assessments of teaching are an important measure of good teaching,** there are some studies of teaching performance over time (Bausell, Schwartz, and Purohit, 1975; Felder and Blackburn, 1981; Hogan, 1973; Smith, 1979). The span, however, is short, the longest being only three years (Felder and Blackburn, 1981). All studies demonstrate a stability over time (that is, observed fluctuations can be attributed to error variance. The one study which probes teaching over the better part of a career (Baldwin and Blackburn, 1981) contains some clues indicating that interest and concern regarding teaching do change. The evidence, however, is anecdotal and not verified with respect to performance.

There are a few cross sectional studies of teaching performance and age. Centra and Zinn's (1976) shows lower ratings for older faculty. Blackburn's (1972) and Hitch's (1980) show distributions resembling a megaphone — more variance at older ages than younger but with correlations near zero. None of these plots suggest career phases. Furthermore, one must have serious reservations about cross sectional data, especially for trying to establish career phases in teaching (Bess, 1973; Riley and others, 1972).

The conclusion from direct evidence, then, is that there are not career phases in the motivation to teach. On the other hand, in the absence of a purposeful test of this proposition, one is reluctant to close the books. The assumptions made above are open to challenge and the existing data are not in the form one might desire.

---

*A *phase* is defined here as a period of time over which a set of values and activities are held relatively constant. *Phase* represents an indefinite interval whose duration is appreciably greater than moment-to-moment or day-to-day. It is more likely at least a year long and more often at least 3 to 5 years in length. A phase can be identified by plotting a professors's performance against time. The interval over which a performance level increases (or decreases) either rather steadily or jumps (falls) rather abruptly and then holds constant constitutes a phase. A change of direction (increase or decrease) marks the onset of a new phase. *Phase* is like *stage* as used by Levinson and others (1978) in its being a distinctive and identifiable condition, one which could be otherwise. It differs from Levinson's *stage* in that it has no necessary developmental components nor is it predicted to occur chronologically.

**Student rating instruments have high reliability coefficients and the rating correlates positively with learning, 0.43 in Cohen's (1980) meta-analysis.

Indirect Evidence

An indirect approach to the problem is to examine evidence regarding the existence of career phases in the other academic roles. The roles are correlated (slightly) so that the appearances of phases in one could support an inference that they also exist in teaching.

Service. Studies on faculty participation in administrative duties (Willie and Stecklin, 1981) and governance (Mortimer, 1969) show an increase in this role with age. They do not, however, display any phases. The one large-scale study on faculty consulting is cross sectional (Lanning and Blackburn, 1978). It shows a rise to a peak and then a decline towards retirement, with variation by discipline and degree of time given to consulting (four levels, including no consulting at all, a category composing about 50 percent of U.S. academics. In conclusion, the meager evidence from the service role does not support the existence of career phases.

Research. Both longitudinal (Pelz and Andrews, 1976; Cole, 1979) and cross sectional (Bayer and Dutton, 1977; Blackburn, Behymer, and Hall, 1978) studies of faculty publications show career phases, at least in the natural and social sciences. While there seem to be differences between disciplines (see especially Bayer and Dutton, 1977), and while there are some discrepancies between longitudinal and cross sectional outcomes (particularly mathematicians—see Cole, 1979; Allison and Stewart, 1974) and between studies using different dependent measures of scholarly productivity, there do seem to be career phases—an early rise, a fall, another rise, and then a dropping off.

There are, however, two difficulties to be faced before inferring phases in faculty motivation to teach from these findings. First, while the correlation studies between student judged teaching effectiveness and different measures of faculty scholarly productivity tend to be positive, they are low and account for no more than 10 percent of the variance. Second, the productivity studies are concentrated on faculty in research universities, institutions which house but a small fraction of the 600,000 teaching faculty. Therefore, a statement asserting the existence of career phases in faculty motivation to teach cannot be supported by the existing evidence.

References

Allison, P. D., and Stewart, J. A. "Productivity Differences Among Scientists: Evidence for a Cumulative Advantage." *American Sociological Review,* 1974, *39* (21), 596–606.
Baldwin, R. G., and Blackburn, R. T. "The Academic Career as a Developmental Process: Implications for Higher Education." *Journal of Higher Education,* 1981, *52* (6), 598–614.
Bausell, R. B., Schwartz, S., and Purohit, A. "An Examination of the Conditions Under Which Various Student Rating Parameters Replicate Across Time." *Journal of Educational Measurement,* 1975, *12* (4), 273–280.

98

Bayer, A. E., and Dutton, J. E. "Career Age and Research-Professional Activities of Academic Scientists: Tests of Alternative Nonlinear Models and Some Implications for Higher Education Faculty Policies." *Journal of Higher Education,* 1977, *48* (3), 259–282.

Bess, J. L. "Integrating Faculty and Student Life Cycles." *Review of Educational Research,* 1973, *43,* 377–403.

Blackburn, R. T. *Tenure: Aspects of Job Security on the Changing Campus.* Atlanta, Ga.: Southern Regional Education Board, Research Monograph, No. 19, July 1972.

Blackburn, R. T., Behymer, C. E., and Hall, D. E. "Research Note: Correlates of Faculty Publications." *Sociology of Education,* 1978, *15,* 132–141.

Centra, J. A., and Zinn, R. L. "Student Points of View in Ratings of College Instruction." *Educational and Psychological Measurement,* 1976, *36* (3), 693–703.

Cohen, P. A. "A Meta-Analysis of the Relationship Between Student Ratings of Instruction and Student Achievement." Unpublished doctoral dissertation, University of Michigan, 1980.

Cole, S. "Age and Scientific Performance." *American Journal of Sociology,* 1979, *84* (4), 958–977.

Felder, N., and Blackburn, R. T. "Student Reactions to the Faculty Pedagogical Role." Paper delivered at annual meeting of the American Educational Research Association, Los Angeles, April 1981.

Hitch, E. J. "Similarity of Student Ratings for Instructor and Courses Across Time." Unpublished doctoral dissertation, University of Michigan, 1980.

Hogan, T. P. "Similarity of Student Ratings Across Instructors, Courses, and Time." *Research in Higher Education,* 1973, *1,* 149–154.

Lanning, A. W., and Blackburn, R. T. "Faculty Consulting and *The* Consultant." Paper presented at annual meeting of the American Educational Research Association, Ontario, Canada, April 1978.

Levinson, D. J., Darrow, C. N., Klein, E. B., Levinson, M. H., and McKee, B. *The Seasons of a Man's Life.* New York: Knopf, 1978.

Mortimer, K. P. "Academic Government at Berkeley: The Academic Senate." Unpublished doctoral dissertation, University of California–Berkeley, 1969.

Pelz, D. C., and Andrews, F. M. *Scientists in Organizations.* (Rev. ed.) New York: Wiley, 1976.

Riley, M. W., Johnson, M., Farrer, A., with Nelson, E. E. "Interpretation of Research on Age." In M. W. Riley, M. Johnson, and A. Farrer (Eds.), *Aging and Society,* Vol. 3: *A Sociology of Age Stratification.* New York: Russell Sage, 1972.

Smith, P. L. "The Stability of Teacher Performance in the Same Course Over Time." *Research in Higher Education,* 1979, *11* (2), 153–165.

Willie, R., and Stecklin, J. E. "A Three Decade Comparison of College Faculty Characteristics, Satisfactions, Activities, and Attitudes." Paper presented at national meetings of the Association for Institutional Research, Minneapolis, May 1981.

Robert T. Blackburn is professor at the Center for the Study of Higher Education, the University of Michigan. His research interests presently center on the examination of academic careers.

The task is to create conditions where faculty see teaching as an opportunity for effort and achievement and an avenue for continued growth and development.

The Motivation to Teach: Meanings, Messages, and Morals

James L. Bess

To enable faculty to recognize the potential of the rewards of teaching requires a conceptualization of the nature of the rewards, identification of the paths by which the rewards can be transmitted, and an understanding of the dynamics of the learning processes by which faculty are enabled to be receptive to the transmitted rewards. As has been pointed out by several of the previous authors, rewards can be classified as intrinsic or extrinsic. We discuss both in terms of their potential for attracting faculty to teaching.

Intrinsic rewards are perceived as pleasurable psychological states. Hackman and Oldham (1980) note that there are at least three such states:

> Experienced Meaningfulness of the Work — the degree to which the individual experiences the job as one which is generally meaningful. Does it demand a variety of skills and talents, does it require completion of a whole and identifiable piece of work, and does it have a substantial impact on the lives of other people? These conditions bring "feelings" of *arousal* from rich stimuli, of *competence* in performance, of *closure* or completeness of a work episode, and of *connectedness* with others in society.

J. Bess (Ed.). *New Directions for Teaching and Learning: Motivating Professors to Teach Effectively*, no. 10. San Francisco: Jossey-Bass, June 1982.

Experienced Responsibility for Work Outcomes—the degree to which the individual feels personally accountable and responsible for the results of the work he or she does. Does the work provide autonomy in task performance? If yes, the work will provide "feelings" of *control* over one's environment.

Knowledge of Results—the degree to which the individual knows and understands on a continuous basis how effectively he or she is performing on the job. Are there built-in and informal feedback mechanisms? When there are, the individual will experience "feelings" of *pleasure* at achievement.*

Whether or not workers achieve these valued inner states is dependent to a large degree on conditions of work which are subject to design by administrators (for example, those in the Galbraith model described by Hall and Bazerman in Chapter 7 of this volume) task, structure, and information and decision process variables.

With respect to higher education, if faculty are expected to experience positive affect as a result of their teaching experience—affect which functions as a reinforcing incentive for further efforts in teaching—then they must be enabled to achieve these three psychological states. Understanding the modes by which faculty may pursue appropriate routes to self-recognition of the states depends in turn on the particular perspective one brings to the conception of motivation.

Let us look, for example, at the intrinsically rewarding states proposed by Hackman and Oldham and ask whether faculty are likely to see them as valuable and forthcoming from the teaching act. Given the almost universal need of people to experience arousal, competence, closure, connectedness, control, and pleasure at achievement, it would be unusual to expect faculty to disregard or devalue these feelings. Certainly, we might surmise that faculty by inclination, socialization, and professionalization would come to view these states as highly desirable results of their professional efforts. This may be in some contrast to workers in other occupations who do not view work as a central life interest, but rather more instrumentally as a means to other ends. It is important, however, to be much more task specific in this instance. Does teaching itself provide for faculty members intrinsically rewarding psychological states? More precisely stated, if faculty are not necessarily intrinsically rewarded from teaching, what is the likelihood of their acting as if their efforts will lead to pleasurable psychological states (to whatever degree they are desired)?

Let us discuss each of the three states separately. With respect to experienced meaningfulness of work as already noted, there are some questions about whether what one does in preparation for teaching will result in good

*Italicized concepts are not in the original Hackman and Oldham definitions.

teaching (in part because faculty are not sure what good teaching is). In addition, the looseness of the causal chain between faculty effort and student gains and the presence of so many other variables contributing to the education of young people causes great, if latent, doubt in faculty that their teaching does make a difference in the lives of the large majority of their students (Cohen, 1973). Hence, faculty are left with only a hope that what they are doing in class is, in fact, meaningful (though they will, of course, initially assert unequivocally that it is so).

A similar argument holds for the second of the psychological states — experienced responsibility for work outcomes. While faculty do have autonomy in the classroom and academic freedom in general, their responsibility over student performance is at least in part a function of student abilities and dispositions and institutional resources (as Mowday notes). Moreover, there is little accountability involved in teaching. Faculty are generally not monitored, nor held accountable for poor performance (unless it is egregiously so). While in earlier chapters several authors cautioned that increases in accountability to others might lead to decreases in faculty motivation, there is reason to believe that the general absence of a norm of self-accountability will lead not only to desultory performance but to the absence of positive affect. As Pelz and Andrews note, complete autonomy without some constraints, either bureaucratic or normative, results in lowered productivity. Finally, the sense of responsibility extends to poor as well as good performance. Hence, autonomy in work cuts two ways and will be psychologically functional in moderate amounts, only if high quality performance is forthcoming. These conditions lead one to believe that faculty will not experience the psychological satisfaction of having control over their environments by virtue of their teaching activities. They will assign low probabilities to the relationship between their autonomous performance and the intrinsic outcome (or psychological state) of experienced responsibility for work outcomes.

The third psychological state — knowledge of results — translates more readily into the pleasure of achievement. The question, then, is the degree to which faculty are likely to assign high probability to the relationship between performance and the feeling of achievement through teaching. As noted earlier, the ambiguity of the results of teaching — if not the lack of success — may force faculty to be less optimistic about the potential for gratification through this channel.

We have been discussing so far the nature of intrinsic rewards, as these may be sources of motivation for faculty. Expectancy theory would appear to demonstrate that teaching as now conceived and practiced in colleges and universities will not yield intrinsic rewards of sufficient magnitude to sustain faculty motivation. But it is conceivable that expectancy theory places too much emphasis on cognition in understanding motivation for that to be a completely satisfactory model. Indeed, as Mowday points out, expectancy theory is most useful in predicting behavior in novel situations, not those which are routine and evoke habitual performance. Let us turn, therefore, to need theory, as outlined by Schneider and Zalesny's chapters, since it stresses another kind of internal energy, stemming, in part, from drive theory.

In need theory, the satisfaction of basic needs releases the individual to seek higher order needs. Here, then, need, instead of extrinsic or intrinsic reward or psychological state, is posed as the force which impels activity. Thus, where conditions permit people (especially those with strong achievement needs) to succeed at moderately challenging and risky tasks, motivation will be sustained. Mature adults, treated as adults, will naturally seek to satisfy their ego and fulfillment needs. Using need theory, we can ask the question whether faculty are likely to be motivated by the opportunities in teaching.

Schneider and Zalesny, in their chapter, make the point that faculty are attracted to the profession because it appears to fit their needs for challenge, opportunity for achievement, and general lack of structure (see Oldham and Hackman, 1980, 1981; Nadler and Tushman, 1977). While empirical evidence on the sources of the image of the profession to prospective faculty is dated and limited, it is reasonable to believe that the socialization and professionalization processes in undergraduate and graduate school incline the would-be faculty toward the profession largely because its research and publication opportunities and concomitant rewards meet those needs. In that case, it follows that teaching tasks may be perceived during early faculty career years as overly challenging and risky, leading in turn to high anxiety and, ultimately, poor performance. (Doubtless, specific anxieties about teaching are buried in the generalized trauma of the pretenure competition.)

The challenge is seen as overwhelming to new faculty in part because the goals of teaching are ineffable and, consequently, soon appear unachievable to young faculty. And teaching is risky, especially to new faculty, because it forces them to demonstrate a competency for which they have had no training. What does need for achievement mean to a person who does not understand what achievement in teaching is? What is the effect on motivation? There is some considerable literature on performance under conditions of high and low challenge and risk, and it is clear that faculty behavior follows closely the predictions of the theories. Faculty are forced to make an adjustment in their perception of the situation and/or in their investment of energy in the activity. As Atkinson (1957) observed, high nAch people prefer intermediate, not high risk ventures. Hence, the likelihood is that faculty will discount the risk in teaching and reinterpret the teaching role, and/or they will put less effort into the teaching activities. While teaching can be conceived as a "developmental" opportunity, to use the Schneider and Zalesny model, it may be that young faculty are unable to view it in those terms, both because of its high risk and because of other, more salient, and apparently more attractive academic tasks.

Some of the authors in the previous chapters argue that extrinsic rewards will diminish intrinsic motivation. It would appear, however, that the relationship between the two depends heavily on whether teaching is or is not perceived by the faculty member as a satisfying (read, "intrinsically rewarding") activity. For example, if faculty are satisfied with teaching, then the danger from heavy doses of extrinsic rewards may, as McKeachie and Deci and Ryan note, result in a diminution of motivation. The reason is that the additional external rewards may be perceived as compensatory — as the overjustification theorists (Lepper and Greene, 1978) tell us — and faculty may come to see such external rewards as payment for unpleasant activity. Thus, teaching may be seen as an undesirable task, and faculty capacity to appreciate the opportunities in the teaching environment for growth, excitement and intrinsic satisfaction may, therefore, be severely diminished.

The preceding scenario is based on the assumption that most faculty do presently find teaching satisfying — a position thus far without systematic empirical justification. Suppose teaching for most faculty is *not* satisfying. What will be the effect of large amounts of external inducements on their motivation to teach? In this case, extrinsic rewards may provide the "hygienic" conditions (to use Herzberg's 1966 term) which prevent aggregate dissatisfactions from interfering psychologically with the climate for investment in teaching. (Though the satisfaction and dissatisfaction dimensions are allegedly independent, recent research by Hoy and Miskel, 1978, seems to indicate that there are some interaction effects.) In other words, when administrators assume (correctly or incorrectly) that faculty do not and cannot find intrinsic satisfactions from teaching, the express use of extrinsic rewards will serve only to prevent faculty *dis*satisfaction with teaching (provided such rewards are widely distributed). Except for those faculty who are constitutionally *contra*-disposed to teaching, as Nord observes, extrinsic rewards will not motivate. In short, extrinsic rewards will keep faculty from becoming overly frustrated with what they perceive is an unpleasant activity and will perpetuate the belief that teaching cannot be intrinsically rewarding.

It is useful at this point to join two of the arguments noted and ask the question as to whether faculty as a whole are dispositionally more risk-taking than the norm for the population as a whole and what effect risk-taking propensities have on their receptivity to extrinsic and intrinsic rewards. Again, research evidence is lacking, but (as noted in the Editor's Notes in this sourcebook) it is reasonable to assume that faculty as a rule are conservative by nature (an hypothesis with which not all of the authors in this sourcebook would agree). Faculty have been socialized in graduate school to the pattern of skepticism which renders all judgments tentative until extensively validated through scientific method and/or consensus in peer review. They risk little opprobrium in publication (those relatively few who do publish), since the editorial screening process usually anonymously filters out the obviously unsound or trivial. Given this orientation, it may be more likely that faculty members will be receptive to hygiene factors more than to motivators (Williams, 1965).

If, then, administrators do begin increasingly to use extrinsic rewards, faculty are quite likely to find them salient. As in the manner of union workers in blue collar jobs, they will find their energies engaged in maximizing these rewards, distracting them from seeing the possibilities for intrinsic satisfactions. (See the discussion in Porac and Salancik, 1981, on the interaction effects of multiple extrinsic rewards.) Thus, if faculty are basically unsatisfied with teaching rewards and if they are, indeed, relatively low risk takers, the provision of external rewards will do nothing but reduce their dissatisfaction without motivating them to teach well. If faculty *are* satisfied and risk-taking, extrinsic rewards may cause them to question the validity of their intrinsic satisfactions, thereby turning faculty toward hygienic factors in their work environments.

It is, of course, unlikely that without some modicum of extrinsic rewards (monetary or social), faculty motivation will be sustained, except in the case of the most exceptional and highly achievement oriented, with extraordinary interests in the teaching domain—those who have come to see teaching as a prime source of satisfaction. In sum, the additive or multiplicative character of extrinsic and intrinsic rewards will apply to faculty motivation to teach only when faculty are strongly oriented toward teaching and when extrinsic rewards are moderate. If faculty are unsatisfied with teaching, the increase in extrinsic rewards will be counterproductive.

This discussion embraces much of the controversy found in the discussions of the relationships among intrinsic and extrinsic rewards and faculty needs for achievement. Another perspective on the subject is presented in the Nord chapter on behavior modification (B-mod) and it, too, is helpful in understanding the faculty member as teacher. Under this conceptualization, the impulse to activity is a function of prior learned connections between certain actions and the pleasurable (or unpleasurable) states which occurred concurrently or soon thereafter. B-mod is also useful in identifying the conditions of work which may lead to pleasurable associations between tasks performed and the feelings which accompany or follow from them (in Nord's terms, the ecological design). The assumption is that a faculty member will repeat behavior which is found to be pleasurable and that if the behavior is also institutionally desirable, it is in the interests of all to encourage it. As with the perspective of the other theories, we can, using B-mod, follow well the reasons why teaching is not pursued as assiduously as it might be by faculty. Again, we can see how the faculty member who has found little or no pleasure from the teaching act will be inclined to extinguish that behavior. Lacking reinforcement, there is little incentive to continue, save in the minimum acceptable modes dictated by institutional and peer standards.

Finally, we turn to a fourth way of explaining the motivation of faculty—or lack of it. Csikszentmihalyi suggests that "flow" experience is a "deep, spontaneous involvement with the task at hand. In flow, one is carried away by interaction, to the extent that one feels immersed in the activity—the distinction between 'I' and 'it' becomes irrelevant." In addition, there is little worry about the adequacy of performance—the intimacy of the involvement in the work provides sensitive feedback so that one moderates one's behavior intuitively as dictated by the nature of the situation and one's competency. There is a balance of challenge and skills. Many of us have experienced this feeling — on occasion. Seldom is it a feature of teaching every day. Why?

Csikszentmihalyi indicates that one reason is that we have the wrong conception of the goals of education. They should involve not the transmission of information but the personification of the meaning of being an alive, curious, and learning adult. Faculty, however, who have modeled their behavior on their own faculty mentors do not see this as responsible teaching. Nor does an academic system which emphasizes the importance of transmitting information. Even in more enlightened educational environments, where liberal education still lives, distribution requirements and coverage of required material constrain faculty to follow standard formats and techniques of teaching. This is not to say that the goals of liberal education must be abandoned, only that the pedagogies associated with it have prevented faculty from realizing the potential of the flow experience in the teaching setting.

In each of these theories — expectancy, need, B-mod, and flow — we find some wisdom. They help to explain why faculty in higher education are not motivated to teach. They reveal why faculty come to see the teaching environment as not providing the opportunities for satisfactions which will justify the exertion of effort and energy. But the theories also point cogently to ways in which the ecology of teaching can be improved so that faculty will become increasingly aware of the potential of the environment and will, indeed, seek satisfactions through teaching. What is required is a change in the climate for teaching as well as a change in the perception of the teaching situation by faculty.

The key lies in the observation of Galbraith (as outlined by Hall and Bazerman) that under conditions of uncertainty, more information must be processed in order for the task to be performed effectively. Since we no longer have bountiful resources, we must, according to the model, develop our capacity for improving information flow. We must improve the vertical flow of information as well as establish more lateral relationships. We must create, through organizational design, systems which "naturally" support teaching through the formal structure of authority and rewards and through the infrastructure of the informal organization and the student culture. The pattern of differentiation and integration of the tasks which comprise the entire range of faculty activities bears importantly on the efficiency of flow of information and rewards (Bess, 1982). While a faculty segregated into teachers and researchers may permit more supportive systems of information and reward, an even more disaggregated task and role structure may be called for — one which better matches faculty preference to organizational requirements. The great variety of teaching tasks (lecturing, advising, tutoring, and so on) calls for a variety of individual dispositions, even as these may or may not change over the faculty career, as Blackburn observes. And we have only begun to understand the organizational structures which can be designed to suit both faculty and institutional needs simultaneously.

But it is not only macro-organizational redesign which is needed. Clearly, the internal dynamics involved in the administration of rewards is critical. As Deci and Ryan point out, rewards delivered in a controlling rather than an informational way will decrease intrinsic motivation. Rewards must be carefully allocated in ways which help faculty members reveal to themselves the competencies which are believed to be important. As Cammann notes, the feedback system must consider the teacher as primary recipient and must use the teacher's own definition of effectiveness in providing timely and appropriate information. The objective of external rewards used in a feedback framework should be to reinforce the teacher's own sense of personal capacity to master a challenging and risky situation. Cammann points out, in addition, that the feedback system must be rich and inventive. Administrators seeking to design a feedback system which is responsive to the complexity of the teaching act must be enormously imaginative to capture its subtleties and nuances. As Weick (1978) has noted, the crucial ingredient in leadership is the nature of the media used to connect the actor to the sensor. Leaders who wish to be effective must, at least initially, be "externally constrained." They must put themselves in positions to be exposed to faculty needs with respect to teaching. Not only must they feed information back to the faculty to reinforce the sense of competence in teaching, but effective leaders will provide rewards which are responsive to the particularistic idiosyncrasies of the faculty member. As Nord suggests, administrators might well ask teachers what they would like and use the requested rewards as reinforcers.

Indeed, researchers might also turn more attention to faculty and the institutions in which they serve as objects of close study. As the literature cited in this volume documents, the studies of individual motivation and organization which have arisen from such studies could obviously gain from special studies of academic behavior as well as contribute to applications as practical as increasing a faculty's motivation to teach. We know that universities will never succeed in achieving their highest, albeit pluralistic, aims with workers who are only partially committed to the enterprise. The task is to create conditions where faculty see teaching as an opportunity for effort and achievement, as a channel for productivity, and as an avenue for experiencing meaningfulness and responsibility. Only then can they, their institutions, and the society at large have any hope of becoming fulfilled.

References

Atkinson, J. W. "Motivational Determinants of Risk-Taking Behavior." *Psychological Review*, 1957, *64*, 359–372.

Bess, J. L. *University Organization, A Matrix Analysis of the Academic Professions.* New York: Human Sciences Press, 1982.

Cohen, A. M. "Toward a Professional Faculty." In A. M. Cohen (Ed.), *New Directions for Community Colleges: Toward a Professional Faculty*, no. 1. San Francisco: Jossey-Bass, 1973.

Hackman, J. R., and Oldham, G. R. *Work Redesign.* Reading, Mass.: Addision-Wesley, 1980.

Herzberg, F. *Work and the Nature of Man.* Cleveland: World, 1966.

Hoy, W. K., and Miskel, C. G. *Educational Administration: Theory, Research, and Practice.* New York: Random House, 1978.

Lepper, M. R., and Greene, D. "Overjustification Research and Beyond: Toward a Means-End Analysis of Intrinsic and Extrinsic Motivation." In M. R. Lepper and D. Greene (Eds.), *The Hidden Costs of Reward: New Perspectives on the Psychology of Human Motivation.* Hillsdale, N.J.: Erlbaum, 1978.

Nadler, D. A., and Tushman, M. L. "A Diagnostic Model for Organizational Behavior." In J. R. Hack, E. E. Lawler III, and L. W. Porter (Eds.), *Perspectives on Behavior in Organizations.* New York: McGraw-Hill, 1977.

Oldham, G. R., and Hackman, J. R. "Work Design in the Organizational Context." *Research in Organizational Behavior,* 1980, *2,* 247–278.

Oldham, G. R., and Hackman, J. R. "Relationships Between Organizational Structure and Employee Reactions: Comparing Alternative Frameworks." *Administrative Science Quarterly,* 1981, *26* (1), 66–83.

Pelz, D. C., and Andrews, F. M. "Autonomy, Coordination, and Stimulation, in Relation to Scientific Achievement." *Behavioral Science,* 1966, *11* (2), 89–97.

Porac, J. F., and Salancik, G. R. "Generic Overjustification: The Interaction of Extrinsic Rewards." *Organizational Behavior and Human Performance,* 1981, *27* (2), 197–212.

Weick, K. "The Spines of Leaders." In M. W. McCall, Jr. and M. Lombardo (Eds.), *Leadership, Where Else Can We Go?* Durham, N.C.: Duke University Press, 1978.

Williams, L. K. "Some Correlates of Risk Taking." *Personnel Psychology,* 1965, *18,* 297–309.

James L. Bess is professor of higher education,
New York University.

Index